PRAISE FOR

KNOWN

Angie eloquently weaves together two stories in this book. She knits together the story of Moses as he leads the Israelites in the book of Exodus and her own story to illustrate her topics. Angie speaks of two types of knowledge: God knowing us and us knowing God. Angie illustrates two paths: the beautiful path God leads us on and the reckless path that we choose aside from God. Angie writes of two ways to direct our focus: direct our attention to the Most High God or center our attention on ourselves and our desires. In the end, Angie speaks of two worships: the worship of the glory of God or elevating ourselves to receive glory. With great skill, deep knowledge of the Word of God, and an understanding of the frailty of the human heart she leads the reader to a right response despite the many barriers we face on the journey of life. The right response is penned in her opening poem in the last line of the third stanza: "Living solely to serve you (Jesus) with every draw of my breath."

— **Cindy Stone,** *Disciple of Jesus Christ*

Angie's God-given ability to put heart language into words is remarkable. The pages of this book are saturated with the beautiful, timely truths of God's Word that can only be soaked up by those whose hearts are empty and ready to go deeper in knowing God and being known by Him.

— **Yiniva Brandon,** *Leader in Women's Ministry and Follower of Jesus Christ*

Angie "keeps it real" as she travels through Exodus and teaches us what it means to know the Lord and to discover that we are fully known too. She helps us find ourselves in both the strengths and weaknesses of Moses and the Israelites. She courageously lets us in to the places of insecurity and doubt in her own story and leaves us hopeful that the holy God of the Bible delights in His children and uses us in spite of our imperfections. This book is thoughtful, relatable, and applicable, but, most of all, its pages are bravely written straight from the heart of a woman who has encountered The Great I Am.

— **Jamie Fuller**, *Friend and Leader in Women's Ministry*

Angela did a wonderful job weaving scriptural stories and truths together in *Known*. From examples like Moses and the Israelites to Adam and Eve, *Known* helps readers learn from the many ways the Lord has been leading Angela on a spiritual journey and transforming her to become more like Christ. In a Pause to Praise and Ponder at the end of each chapter, readers are encouraged to not only apply the chapter's material to their own lives but also to enjoy getting creative alongside the Lord.

— **Hilary Bernstein**, *Women's Ministry Director at The Chapel in Green*

Known is a compelling book for anyone who wants to know God for who He is and is ready to let go of the box they've put Him in. Angela writes with honest rejections, bringing the familiar story of Exodus into new light as she connects it beautifully to our own faith journeys. Through her thoughtful questions and vulnerable prayers, you'll quickly begin to see how seeking to know His voice (John 10:27) and recognizing the lies that compete with it is truly where you come to be known by God and discover your purpose in life. As a pastor, I highly recommend this book and already can't wait to have it on my shelf to hand to those who step into my office.

— **Brett Faris,** *Pastor of Care, The Chapel in Green*

KNOWN

OUR GOD-ORDAINED JOURNEY THROUGH THE WILDERNESS

ANGELA GUY

Published by KHARIS PUBLISHING,
an imprint of KHARIS MEDIA LLC.

ISBN-13: 9781637466810
ISBN-10: 1-63746-681-1
Library of Congress Control Number:

Kharis Media LLC
Tel: 1-630-909-3405
support@kharispublishing.com
www.kharispublishing.com

CONTENTS

1

THE BEAUTIFUL PATH

Jesus, You know every move that the enemy makes.
You are so aware of each action the enemy takes.
You hear each cry made in misery and desperation.
Your rescue reaches out to us, O God of creation.
Nestled safely in You, through the flood of the Father's wrath,
Jesus, You lead your people on a beautiful path.
You are my pillar of strength. You came down and lit the way.
Surely Your goodness and mercy follow me every day.

O beautiful path leading me to the Promised Land.
O beautiful path that tests me in a dry wasteland.
O beautiful path, an escape on a narrow road.
O beautiful path, where mercy and abundance flow.

Scared to embrace the unknown, distress makes us hasty.
We look to the past with longing, so eager for safety.
O God, be my strength; staunch this flow of traitorous thoughts
That dares to reduce your goodness to what this world allots.
Show me that my slavery is gone. Highlight its brevity.
Remove the pain of my past that seems to wound endlessly.

Even in this desert, I will abundantly succeed.
Though my hands are empty, God, your presence is all I need.

O beautiful path leading me to the Promised Land.
O beautiful path that tests me in a dry wasteland.
O beautiful path, an escape on a narrow road.
O beautiful path, where mercy and abundance flow.

Teach me to follow you out of the boat and on to the sea.
Show me that when I am drowning you will always reach me.
Teach me to follow you into the shadowy valleys,
That your protection extends to the darkest of alleys.
Teach me how to enter the furnace; the heat has increased.
I know you enter in with me, my marvelous High Priest.
Teach me to follow you, bearing my cross unto death.
Living solely to serve you with every draw of my breath.

O beautiful path leading me to the Promised Land.
O beautiful path that tests me in a dry wasteland.
O beautiful path, an escape on a narrow road.
O beautiful path, where mercy and abundance flow.

Have you ever noticed how much easier it is to see the handprint of God after events have occurred, compared to how easy it is to sense His direction during the chaos, the problems, and the choices before us? In the moment, you cannot see the stringing together of events and how those strung events lead us through the course of our lives for a distinct purpose. In retrospect, I can see God guiding me so clearly that it baffles me that I did not notice His leading at the time. Amazingly, as I reflect, even in times of overtly rigid obstinance on my part, when my eyes were squeezed tightly shut in my refusal to look towards God and my fingers were jammed in my ears to stop His voice from coming through, He was working to lead my heart back to Himself. Although I long to be faithful and loyal, my walk has been filled with wandering and returning. My eyes have been opened to just how often my desire to serve Him ends with selfishly seeking my own glory. Yet without fail, God leads me back to repentance and gratitude for His never-ending grace.

God makes it clear that I am not alone in my struggle. The Bible reflects mankind's repetitious waywardness and God's loving pursuit of us to bring us into reconciliation with Him. This story is the same throughout history. Nothing is new under the sun (Ecclesiastes 1:9). God's plans have always been to bless us (Genesis 1:28), but we either doubt Him or we reject His ways. God provides and sustains life, and His creation is good (Genesis 1:31), but humanity is not satisfied with God's provision. God provides instruction that teaches selfless love and righteousness. Meanwhile, humanity rebels, perceiving an unreasonable rigidity in God and accusing Him of restricting our rights with stifling rules and an unwillingness to accept us. Dissatisfied with God's ways, we choose to decide for ourselves what is good and right. We have set our eyes upon what we desire, and what we desire benefits us: power, control, possession of good things, and self-sufficiency. Violence results, and the result of this violence is the reaping of more violence. We wander further from God and His intent for His creation. Goodness dissipates and soon disappears. Things get darker and bleaker. We become blind and broken without hope.

I marvel at the lives, described within the Bible, of the men and women who obeyed God's voice and stepped out in faith. Do their lives stir something within you, or do the mighty acts in the Bible feel too far removed from your life and how God moves today? Do their lives make you long to allow God to do mighty things through you, or do they make you squirm a bit, preferring that God skip over you when He doles out these sorts of tasks? Maybe there is a little bit of each of these feelings within all of us. We long to have a purpose and make a difference, to have value and worth, yet fear or preoccupation with ourselves makes us seek to avoid it. Moses is one of these obedient, faithful figures for me. When I take in the purposes of God that he fulfilled, I recognize what a blessed life he lived. Imagine being selected by God to rescue over 600,000 people from 430 years of slavery. What a life of abundance he lived to guide all of God's people for so many years, shepherding them not only towards the Promised Land but also toward God's heart.

Then my zeal to be like Moses dissipates when I consider the details of his life, the hardships, and the sacrifices of not growing up with his family but in a foreign house. What made Moses look towards his people instead of standing firm in Pharaoh's household? What drove him to look toward a group of slaves and intercede on their behalf? Was it solely compassion or was he a bit of an outcast who experienced loneliness and isolation, knowing he didn't belong? Then, after taking matters into his own hands, he was forced from the only home he ever knew into the wilderness, running for fear of his life. We get a glimpse into his difficulties when we read that he named his son Gershom, a name which meant "sojourner in a foreign land" (Exodus 2:22). It speaks of loneliness, and I relate to him. I long for just a little bit more detail into his emotional state. In the wilderness, this man who was displaced since infancy finally finds belonging and contentment with a family of his own. He is then sent back to rescue his people and live out the remainder of his days wandering the wilderness with them complaining and being stiff-necked, only to never actually step foot into the Promised Land on account of his own anger (Numbers 20:10–12). What sounds like an amazing accomplishment does not seem very glamorous in detail at all, does it?

Like Moses, I fled the difficulties of my past and was living in hiding. As I was nearing forty, I looked around and realized how tired I was of being incapacitated because of my fears and doubts. I was weary of toiling, trying to be better and consistently failing. My heart was primed and ready. I was nearing the end of myself but was not yet willing to let go of my desires. I did not want to lay down my life to fully yield to the ways of Jesus, but I was being drawn to Him. I began a Bible study in the book of John. Two verses in chapter 10 related to transformation, which caused a stirring within me, which led to a yearning in my heart, have remained with me. They are John 10:10: "The thief comes only to steal and kill and destroy. I came that they may have life and have it abundantly," and John 10:27: "My sheep hear my voice, and I know them, and they follow me."

I was intrigued by this life of abundance God promises and so began a search to understand what a true life of abundance looks like. I knew imitation abundance and how it requires more and more to be enough, and how, with full hands and a full schedule, somehow you remain just as empty as before. I understood how, initially, it feels wonderful, so you grasp ahold of it, and it ultimately robs you of satisfaction, joy, and rest. I began praying to God to show me His life of abundance, and I quickly discovered that godly abundance is not worldly abundance, and that godly abundance begins with letting go of the desire to obtain worldly treasure. Yet even as I went through the hardship and want, I came to understand that God was the one leading me. I discovered that I never felt more alive than when I heard God's voice, when I knew I heard it, and when I followed it in obedience. God took situations that I did not necessarily want to be in and orchestrated these lovely moments of community with Him, moments of learning to trust Him. So began an authentic desire to know God and to daily hear His voice. I became resolute in my request to God to know Him and be changed by Him.

When I began actively seeking to hear God's voice, I discovered something very quickly. God does not direct every step loudly and clearly. At times, I felt compelled to act with a certainty that God is calling me to something specific. At other times, as I listened and waited expectantly, I saw Him guiding me down a path without specific, detailed direction. It was more like a view of His hand weaving a tapestry of circumstances and events within my life, for His purposes, rather than one definite action of obedience. God not only speaks to me through His Word but He also uses circumstances in my life to grab my attention and people to pour into my life to give me wise counsel. God was teaching me the balance of waiting expectantly on Him while moving in faith. Choosing to wait for a definitive, clear word from Him before moving in faith would have rendered me motionless, and I would have missed beautiful things. I have come to love both forms of communication from my Creator and realize that both test my faith. One is a specific task that He has given me in life to fulfill, and it reinforces who is the Lord of my life. It forces me to answer the question, "Am I willing to obey Your voice?" The other is an invitation to be with Him and to learn more of Him and His ways, and it forces me to answer the question, "Am I willing to move with You because I love You that much— so much that I am concerned with and build my life upon what you love?"

There were times when God was noticeably clear to me without me being able to fully explain it. I just knew He was calling me to act. The Holy Spirit left no room for doubt, and I felt at peace with fulfilling God's call on my life. So, even as the execution was challenging, I did not have to question whether I heard or perceived God correctly. Those tend to be the easier acts of obedience because doubt is one of Satan's biggest weapons in my life. It is a spiral that begins with whether I am hearing God's voice, which leads to doubting my abilities and my worth, taking me to a place of shame. The lie is masked in self-doubt, when at the core, I am doubting God's might and ability to work through me. It is as if I receive an invitation to take part in His work instead of a command to act. I sense God stirring something within me, but He does not always clearly relay how to move. This can involve an added layer of trust because I am venturing forward with an offering, not certain of success, doubting my abilities and questioning my success rate. I am in a place of trying to discern whether hardships related to it are tests from God or closed doors. Yet, in these moments my heart seeks after Him. My head is turned towards Him, and my ears are listening for His voice. During these times of uncertainty, God often draws my attention to something by presenting three separate and distinct happenings in my life that lead to the same message. The consistent message helps me discern how God is inviting me to walk with Him from my random thoughts which are constant in my mind.

While I am no longer so hesitant to move and more confident in discerning God's voice, I am amazed that God often still reveals things to me in threes, continuing the same pattern of speaking, affirming, and then solidifying them as He directs the course of my life. I begin moving when I hear his voice and wait expectantly for His blessed affirmation as He lights the path forward because His grace and His guidance never fail me. I marvel at how the process of teaching others about God's heart continually teaches me even more about His heart. He calls me to move, looking toward the needs of others, and, through the process, gives me a greater understanding of His love for me.

The heart behind this book took shape through the mental ponderings of three separate trains of thought that converged together and, though disjointed and blurry initially, took shape and fit like the pieces of a puzzle. We can begin to obey from a place of confident obedience or a delightful invitation, but we will not fully know what to do until the substance of His calling has taken shape. As Moses discovered, dire consequences result, veering our lives off course, when we move ahead of God in our own might. Even if we know the destination, we are to follow God's path which He lights along the way. God's path is so very different than the path we would choose because God is teaching us to rely on Him while on the journey. Moving in faith without seeing the full picture is often God's way because it tests our faith. We can be so focused on the action or the destination that we cannot see that beauty is most often found in waiting. We not only learn a great deal about our God in the wait but we also discover a great deal about ourselves. Waiting is a fertile ground for learning to know God and be known by Him. Properly waiting, with joy, expectation, and ears ready to hear, creates such an environment of reliance on God. We listen. We do. We wait, and then we do more. I listened. I wrote. I reflected. I waited.

The first train of thought was what to do with my newly burning desire to encourage others to embrace being transformed into the likeness of Christ, to show others the joy contained in living His life of abundance, in hearing God's voice, and in moving in obedience. I have always been quiet, but I was extremely quiet about sharing my faith. It made me so uncomfortable to think I was making others uncomfortable. My presentation of the gospel was almost contritely shared because I knew that people did not want to hear that their best attempts were not enough. As Romans 1:16-17 says, "For I am not ashamed of the gospel, for it is the power of God for salvation to everyone who believes, to the Jew first and also to the Greek. For in it the righteousness of God is revealed from faith for faith, as it is written, 'The righteous shall live by faith.'" Sadly, my desire for my own comfort superseded my concern for the everlasting well-being of others. As God poured into me His grace and mercy, and as I began recognizing how He guided my steps, especially in real time, He became the source of my joy. The burden of doing everything perfectly was lifted and I was able to just follow Him. He was no longer a burden to share. I want everyone to know and experience the joy that I have found. Nothing on this earth and no identity that I could possibly claim comes close to the goodness of being known and claimed by God. He is the Living Water inside of me that gives me life. The more He fills me, the more pours out of me to share with others, because His goodness overflows.

I was asking God for guidance on how to begin, on how to connect with people, and on who to approach. Was I meant to teach others how to disciple, was I to connect with women in my church one-on-one, or was I meant to reach someone in the world? I was told of a newly developing discipleship ministry—there was an invitation extended to me to possibly take part in it—but the ministry itself would not begin for another year. There was no shape behind it or even a real discussion of what role I would play, but my heart was certainly drawn to it. I began praying and listening. The first thing God revealed to me was not what role to take or how to do it but the challenges of reaching out and connecting with people in discipleship. It would be so great if we could follow three simple steps and people would transform into the likeness of Christ by the thousands, but while the message of hope is simple, the process is not. Seeds planted usually soften hearts over time. We cannot *make* people believe or *force* them to submit to God's authority. Belief comes with the awareness and difficult acknowledgement that we are not as "good" as we want to believe we are. It requires an acceptance of the truth of the condition of our hearts, when our hearts long to rage against the truth in defensiveness and belligerence.

Another challenge is that discipleship is relational. There is no perfect method, only a perfect model of patience and love. People are unique. They are at various stages in their lives. For some, we need to welcome, coddle, and feed. For others, we need to challenge, encourage, and release, and with others, we just need to meet them in their pain and suffering. What became clear to me was our need to rely on the Holy Spirit to guide us to speak truth while loving without hypocrisy and with vulnerability. It sounds so simple, yet there is so much to learn to get to a place where we venture forth and speak truth—the right truth that people's hearts need to hear in that moment—without hiding ourselves and our struggles or hiding from the discomfort of the conversation. Our sin nature longs to hide in the darkness. We hide our imperfections from God and others, but God calls us into the light to deliver us. 1 John 1:7 tells us, "But if we walk in the light, as he is in the light, we have fellowship with one another, and the blood of Jesus his Son cleanses us from all sin." If we are not comfortable with one another, if we fear that we will not be met with grace and compassion, if we fear rejection, or if we do not feel seen, known, and accepted, we will never walk through the door of a church nor reveal the worst of ourselves—the hidden ugly of our hearts. As God's ambassadors, our actions should equally reflect God's heart of grace and truth.

Next, He began revealing to me people's barriers to spiritual growth and why we are hesitant to follow God in an unrestrained manner. Being drawn into deeper and deeper intimacy with Him *will* permanently change the course of our lives and what we know. Living for comfort will no longer be an option for our lives. As disciples, we are called to "arise and go" so others are invited to "come and see." The beginning of any of these "calls" to our lives of "come and see," "follow Me," and "arise and go," are wrought with fear and uncertainty, so these are the times when we are in the greatest danger of grasping tightly—holding onto our worldly things, our desires, and what brings us comfort.

The second train of thought was seeking to understand my own personal identity in Christ, what purposes God made *me* specifically for. Psalm 139:16 says, "Your eyes saw my unformed substance; in your book were written, every one of them, the days that were formed for me, when as yet there was none of them." I had just completed my first book and did not know if it would be accepted by a publisher. During the wait, God moved me to step down from almost a decade of service in a specific area of my church. He told me I needed to be ready, but I could not see what for. The timing seemed bizarre. My eyes could not see anything on the horizon to require this urgency. I found myself in a season of waiting. I had just finished the most intense year of schedule navigation: driving four children, three of whom were teenagers, to their various activities, while working outside the home, authoring a book, and serving in my church. At the point of this call to obedience, compared to the insane schedule that I just completed, I felt as if I had a plethora of time. Two of the four teenagers whom I had been driving around now had their driver's licenses. Chauffeuring so many people around was gone, and the book was completed. But it was one of those clear callings, so, I stepped down and I waited. I prayed. I shared my heart with God and asked Him for discipleship opportunities because the desire to disciple people was so constant on my heart. I longed for a ministry of discipleship. A quote from C.S. Lewis sums it up best. "Christianity is a statement which, if false, is of no importance, and if true, of infinite importance. The only thing it cannot be is moderately important."[1] I long to encourage people to recognize how infinitely important the gospel is, instead of continuing to live as if it is moderately important to our lives. I prayed, *Lord, you know what you made me for. You know me.*

1. C. S. Lewis, *God in the Dock,* ed. Walter Hooper (Grand Rapids, MI: Wm. B. Eerdmans Publishing Company, 1970), 101.

Reveal to me my identity in you. The only response I heard was "Authenticity." What does that mean? Authenticity is defined as the quality of being true to oneself, aligning one's actions, thoughts, and beliefs with one's core values and identity, rather than pretending to be someone that one is not. It is being genuine. We think authenticity is responding to how we feel, but that is contrary to the definition of authenticity. We cannot be genuine if we don't understand first how we were designed by God to be. Our authentic identity must come from the One who made us. Instead of answering my question with "what," He answered my question with "how." I thought, *Ok Lord, I am going to keep each of these potential paths open until you completely shut them and whatever I do, I will seek to do it with authenticity and vulnerability no matter the fear, disgrace, or humiliation to myself.* I will freely share my struggles of living out who you made me to be as I often retreat and hide in doubt and fear.

While I waited for God to direct, I considered the desires God had placed on my heart:

1. True connection and encouragement!
2. Discipleship!
3. Authentic transformation!

I thought I would spend the summer authentically connecting with women—seeing them and serving them—to see if any discipleship relationships would grow organically. I knew I could not control anything with the book and, rather than wait in an anxious manner, I would put myself to good use. In my own wisdom, I decided to focus on what I could control and pour into women from my church. Ironically, every avenue of connection—a summer Bible study, a church-appointed mentor-mentee relationship, and even just connecting with friends, which should have been easy—were all closed doors. God was showing me that, in my own power, even the simplest of connections is not possible. This was a beautiful lesson that there is beauty in waiting and that my efforts are futile without God. As Psalm 127:1 says, "Unless the LORD builds the house, those who build it labor in vain. Unless the LORD watches over the city, the watchman stays awake in vain."

Yet the book, a wall I could not breach without God's help, happened with such ease. Doors opened quickly and easily. God took care of everything, a beautiful lesson that everything is possible with God, which I learned while I waited. And then I thought, *So, now what, God? This does not help me know what I need to be ready for. The book is written. Are you telling me that writing is my ministry? Am I to continue writing? Am I even ready to do that? I only have one story, and I already shared it. Most of the positive feedback I received on the book focused on my personal story. Are you saying that there is another book in me? Am I an author who needs inspiration? Am I a mentor in want of a mentee? Am I a teacher of Your Word in want of students?* As I sought God's guidance, I realized that my heart longed for all three to be true. I long to see people transformed by the power and love of Christ, yet no mentee, no student, nor any inspired words were materializing. As I waited, I asked. As I waited, I listened. I journaled and I pondered. I received so many seemingly random thoughts just waiting to be put together.

I did not know where God was leading me, but I did know that these were desires that God had placed in me. For years, I avoided any relational entanglements. I withdrew and hid from people. The rejection, the awkwardness, and the feeling of invisibility were too much for my heart to continually take. My small circle of influence, the bonds I had with my family and few friends were enough for me. Suddenly, I was at the point where I desired to look towards the needs of others, to "arise and go", to actively reach out to people instead of only focusing on how uncomfortable that made me. The inspiration behind what became this book has been ruminating in my mind for a while. I spent years knowing about God, knowing His name, thinking I knew Him when there was little depth and intimacy. It was a time when I did not seek to know Him, even though I claimed Him as my own. Now that He has reclaimed my heart and I know Him more every day, I desire to guide people toward knowing Him as well, to discover how to delight in God's Word and to delight in His ways. I desire for them to relinquish hurts and fears and to trust that God is moving them from pain to purpose, and I desire to see them delight in fulfilling the purposes that He has created specifically for them to accomplish.

I thought, *God, how does this shy, unable-to-relate-well-with-people-person reach people for you?* I know I am not an accident. I know there is purpose and intention behind how I have been uniquely created, but it has taken me many years to move beyond my limitations and reach this point of seeking God in this way. I have seen the truth of 2 Corinthians 1:4, that God is the one "who comforts us in all our affliction, so that we may be able to comfort those who are in any affliction, with the comfort with which we ourselves are comforted by God."

Everything that God has revealed to me over this year of waiting was never intended to puff me up. I am nothing outside of God. Running off and grasping ahold of my identity outside of God is futile and empty. Discovering more about my identity in God has provided healing and a sense of worth that has been amazing to my life, but the end goal is not about me at all. Everything He has shown me is from the perspective of how I am specifically made to further His kingdom because that is what I was made for, to glorify God and edify the church.

The answer to the question of what I was supposed to be ready for came into focus with the addition of the third train of thought, an inductive study on the book of Exodus. As I walked through the chapters, I saw passages that were heavily steeped in the importance of knowing and being known. God repeatedly uses the phrase, "Then you will know that I am the LORD your God." What does knowing God change? For me, knowing God has changed everything. Pharaoh did not know God, and this lack of knowledge drove his evil, violent actions and ultimately led to his demise. Exodus 10:7 illustrates how Pharaoh did not know God nor even understand Him and the consequences for resisting Him in the way that his magicians and other servants did: "Then Pharaoh's servants said to him, 'How long shall this man be a snare to us? Let the men go, that they may serve the LORD their God. Do you not yet understand that Egypt is ruined?'" We are in a world of unknowing people, blindly grasping at false identities all around them. Although they are shrouded in darkness, we are called to shine God's light of truth brightly so others can come to know Him as we know Him.

In Exodus, we learn about a man named Moses who did not know himself. He did not know where he belonged, and this lack of knowledge affected his life choices. It would take most of his life before he became the man that God created him to be. Like Moses, we tend to look at our own limitations instead of looking at and standing firm on God's abilities. Much of my life was spent fleeing from the pain of my past. I hid from people, not engaging them or speaking to them, fearful of rejection and being unseen.

Being invisible by choice was preferable to being ignored when I tried to belong. God calls us out of hiding to a purpose specially made for us to fulfill that will bring Him honor and glory.

While we are blind and unknowing, God knows. The book of Exodus shows that He knows Himself and He knows Moses. God knows His people. God knows the actions of Pharaoh. God teaches Moses and His people to know Him and to learn how to know themselves through Him. My mind was so full of thoughts regarding the "perfect way" to develop a discipleship group, and in my quest for perfection, I missed the most important detail, the Perfect One. My study of Exodus finally clicked the pieces of the puzzle into place. Like Moses, it was as if God was saying to me, "Let me strip you of your serving identity. I am going to let you wander out in the wilderness for a little bit. I will give you glimpses and pieces of what I want from you, but I will not pull it together in deliverance and success until I have worked on your heart for a while. I must teach you who is leading and who is following. I will start with the end. You will know the destination and what it is going to look like but not the steps to get there. You must learn to trust me in the process."

Yes, we will explore topics like barriers to transformation and the need for balance in our lives, but I want to make it clear that no single book or specific Bible study method is "The" game-changing method. Instead of laying out a multi-step, "sure to bring success" formula, we will walk through Exodus and focus our attention on the key to transformation and discipleship: the freedom that comes from not only knowing God but also comes in the security of being known by God, so that without fear we can venture forth to make God known. To know God, we must understand that we are known by God, that no parts of our nature are hidden from Him. All sin is seen by God and covered through Christ, and our weaknesses and inadequacies are as much for His purposes and His plan as our strengths, talents, and abilities.

At times I have included Scripture and at times I notate verses because the details within Scripture are so important. I grew up learning about the stories within the book of Exodus, and I would have told you that I knew this story. When I slowed down, however, and took in the details that are provided, especially in comparison to where detail was lacking, I saw so much more in the narrative that pointed to knowing God, being known by

God, and making God known. I long to share these things with you. I recommend reading the book of Exodus prior to reading or as you read this book. It may even be helpful to begin at Genesis 37 to read through the story of Joseph. The beauty of spending time in God's Word and taking it with you throughout your day by pondering a verse, a word, or a phrase, is that it uncovers new treasures and riches contained within, no matter how many times you have read it before. We will be taking a deep dive into the book of Exodus, discussing things that I have been pondering for years, but we will also come back up to the surface for a breath before we dive back down again. My hope is to create just enough interest that you take a few things with you throughout your day, that you develop a habit of pondering God's Word and making discoveries on your own, and that you discover a deep, abiding thirst for meditating on God's word for the pleasure of knowing Him more. If you are new to pondering, I encourage you to be patient with yourself. Like any discipline, it is something that takes practice and needs to be developed, but the result of hearing God speak to you through His Word, guiding you through your days of want and days of victory, is a priceless treasure.

Whether you feel that you are currently stuck in life or if you are convinced that you are going places, you are on a God-ordained journey. God is moving you and the journey takes time to get to the destination He has in mind, so we benefit from remembering and stopping to reflect on how far we've come and what God has brought us through. Reflection requires patience and trust. God wants us to seek Him and to seek His will through prayer and reading His Word. The simplicity of communicating with God does not have to be boring, however. I found that when I took the time to ponder and meditate on God's Word, that His Word came alive for me. I started to ask questions and reflect on how the God of the Bible that these men of faith wrote about is the same God who protects and provides for me today. I began having fun and started being creative in my time with God. The first thing we discover about God in the Bible is that He is creative, so I encourage you to be creative as God is creative. Journal, write, draw, reflect, lament, make lists, ask questions, write poetry, and engage with God and His Word.

At the end of each chapter, I will include suggested ways you can pause to praise and ponder. Do not worry about whether you are doing the exercise right. The point is to spend time with God, remembering what God has done for you and enjoying His presence. These are merely suggestions of ways to creatively engage and spend time with our Creator and to ponder the text that you have just finished. These exercises will challenge you to reflect, sometimes on yourself, but are not meant to keep us focused on ourselves. The hope is that by reflecting on the reality of our hearts, you will allow God to mine out the ways we do not fully trust Him and ways that we do not live for Him. Part of the process is self-reflection, but God-reflection must be included in the process. We will always begin by focusing on the goodness of God and how you have personally come to know our God in these magnificent ways, and we will end with the goodness of God by reinforcing that He is greater than our sin and our fears. Focus on God and ask Him to search you and you will have community with God that is life-giving. To access printable sheets that correspond to the suggested exercises, go to Abundant Life ministry's website at https://www.alm-thewell.org/wellofcreativity.

The refining process is ever going. It is a continual pattern of learning to trust and letting go, of venturing into the scary and unknown in obedience for the sake of love. Am I going to choose God's way or demand my own way? Will fear win out, or is God, alone, enough for me? Through this purification process, we can come to intimately know the unwavering, steadfast love of our God and Savior through these struggles. Every time there is a battle of wills and we choose our will, God's mercy and forgiveness reign supreme, and we gain that much more assurance that His mercy is never failing, even as we continually fail Him. My heartfelt desire is that all discover the joy and intimacy of knowing and being known by God, that we relinquish the comfortable for a life of extraordinary faith and step into the calling of making God known.

~

PAUSE TO PRAISE AND PONDER:

God took the Israelites on a beautiful path from slavery in Egypt to the Promised Land through a barren, vast wilderness. God could have taken the Israelites straight to the Promised Land, but He chose to take them another way for their own benefit. Does God similarly work in your life today? Exodus 13:17 says, "When Pharaoh let the people go, God did not lead them by way of the land of the Philistines, although that was near. For God said, "Lest the people change their minds when they see war and return to Egypt."

Theme: To recognize that we are on a journey and being led by God. What is your journey?

Praise: How have you seen this Deliverer God who directs our paths in your life? In what ways can you bring Him praise?

Brainstorming: List the major events that have happened in your life to lead you to where you are today.

Mirror: God used the story of the Israelites to show the world that He is a God who delivers His people from slavery. He also shows that He is a God who has a plan that has a path that might not look like the path we would choose.
How is God using your story to show His nature of love and deliverance to the world?
- Reflect on your hardships.
- Reflect on your open doors and unique opportunities.

Ask God to reveal to you how He will use these hardships and open doors for His glory. What fears and failures from your past are holding you back from stepping toward what God has in store for you?

Get Creative:
- Map the major events of your life on a timeline.

- Draw a treasure map. Put major life events on the map with dashed lines linking events together.
- Draw a string of pearls and write how events of your life are strung together.

Daily Bread: In what ways can you bring God praise? How has He been present in the ups and the downs of your life?

- Draw a drinking glass. Select a verse related to what God has revealed to you today as you pondered that speaks truth about the ways and promises of God.
- Draw a sandwich.
    - On the bottom bun, praise God by writing who you know Him to be.
    - Select an aspect of your story that God revealed to you as you pondered, an aspect you need to hand over to Him, and write it in the meat portion of the sandwich.
    - Consider both how you have come to know God and what He reveals about Himself in the Bible. How is God fully able to lead you in this situation? In the top bun, continue to praise God by writing the ways you know God is fully able to lead you in this situation.

2

KINGS AND SLAVES

Exodus 1:8 "*Now there arose a new king over Egypt, who did not know Joseph.*"

Whether from Charlton Heston, *The Prince of Egypt,* or the Bible itself, almost everyone has a visual of the epic story of Exodus, a story that starts with kings and slaves, with the powerful oppressing the weak, stomping them underfoot to further exalt themselves. Most envision the mighty acts that take place within this story like the plagues upon the Egyptians or the parting of the Red Sea. The might of God is certainly at the story's forefront as He brings judgment upon the nation that oppresses and enslaves His people, the Israelites. We cheer knowing that good overcomes evil, but the story itself almost seems fanciful. It seems far removed from how we live and how we see God move today. In some ways, this story seems almost irrelevant to us. Sure, God can still move in these mighty ways, but does He?

What is not likely to come to mind when considering this story is the concept of knowledge or wisdom. Yet the word *know*, in its various tenses, occurs in the book of Exodus over forty times. This theme of knowing, interwoven throughout the pages of this epic story, begins in its very first chapter with the discovery that Pharaoh does not know Joseph. Why was that so significant that it is captured in the Bible? The very first thing that we discover about the king of Egypt *is* his knowledge problem. Then, as the story unfolds, we discover how this knowledge problem has a drastic impact on his life decisions and his choices. This impact is so drastic that we should ask ourselves, "What am I supposed to know from this story? What knowledge am I lacking? What changes would occur in our lives if we kept this knowledge theme in view as we take in the big moments of this story?" Throughout the book of Exodus, we see a myriad of ways that we can experience God personally and hear His voice. We learn of the miracles of God, which leave no doubt of God's authority and power over all creation. We hear the words of God spoken from His own mouth to Moses and uttered by Moses, both as the human author of Exodus and as a character in the story. Moses not only shares what God revealed to him as moments are unfurling, but also his understanding of God in retrospect. Through these various perspectives, Moses explains happenings, and we come to know and understand this God of the Hebrews more deeply because through hard circumstances Moses came to know Him more deeply.

But the dialog of the story begins not with a lack of knowledge of God but a lack of knowledge of Joseph. Joseph was one of the sons of Israel, the great-grandson of Abraham, and a member of the family upon whom God's favor rested. Jealousy caused Joseph's brothers to sell him into slavery for twenty shekels of silver, and Joseph found himself a slave in the foreign land of Egypt. The Egyptians did not worship the God of Israel. They worshipped many gods, including their Pharaoh. During Joseph's life, he was unfairly sold, falsely accused, and unjustly imprisoned. But through it all, God was with him, and God eventually exalted him. The Pharaoh who reigned during the time of Joseph exhibited wisdom. He understood that the God of Joseph was to be revered and honored. He had this to say about Joseph, in Genesis 41:38–40, "And Pharaoh said to his servants, 'Can we find a man like this, in whom is the Spirit of God?' Then Pharaoh said to Joseph, 'Since God has shown you all this, there is none so discerning and wise as you are. You shall be over my house, and all my people shall order themselves as you command. Only as regards the throne will I be greater than you.'"

The Pharaoh who reigned in Exodus 1 did not have the same wisdom and discernment as his predecessor. His lack of knowledge led him to some unbelievably bad choices, choices that were generated from fear and dread and that led to horrific actions. Exodus 1:8-11 tells us, "Now there arose a new king over Egypt, who did not know Joseph. And he said to his people, 'Behold, the people of Israel are too many and too mighty for us. Come, let us deal shrewdly with them, lest they multiply, and, if war breaks out, they join our enemies and fight against us and escape from the land.'" Pharaoh did not know God's people, so he had no care or compassion for their well-being. This powerful "god-king" was ruled by fear but not by the right kind of fear. Pharaoh did not know God, so he did not fear Him as he should. What would the god of this mighty nation have to fear from these people unless he wasn't a real god at all but an imposter god who flaunted himself above God Most High?. This pride and rejection of God's ways allowed him to scheme and justify, oppressing Joseph's descendants instead of honoring them and revering God. His scheming reached such a level of horror that he began to attack Israel's innocent children. Exodus 1:22 recounts, "Then Pharaoh commanded all his people, 'Every son that is born to the Hebrews you shall cast into the Nile, but you shall let every daughter live.'" The hearts of the people followed the heart of their king. Instead of Pharaoh's actions horrifying them, they dreaded the Israelites. Exodus 1:12 tells us, "But the more they were oppressed, the more they multiplied and spread abroad, and the Egyptians were in dread of the people of Israel."

Then Pharaoh died, and a new king came to power, but his choices were no better. He did not relent against the Israelites (Exodus 2:23), so we conclude that he also did not know Joseph. Then, when we see his reaction to Israel's God, we know that he does not know God either. This ruler pridefully claims that he does not know I AM. He stubbornly ignores God's warnings and refuses to yield to Him and to honor Him. He, in stubborn defiance, chooses instead to increase the oppression of God's people.

As I journey in life, learning to submit my ways to Jesus Christ, I still have so much to learn and discover about my King. Like the words spoken of Pharaoh in Exodus 1:8, something similar could be stated of me, "Now there was born a daughter of the God Almighty, who did not intimately and truly know God's Son." I was ruled by fear, driven by my desires, trying harder, doing more, and becoming more deeply invested in my sinful ways.

From the most faithless to the most faithful, we all have one thing in common. We have a knowledge problem. Each of us could benefit from pondering the question, "How might I end up making negative choices because of how little I know Jesus Christ?" Like Joseph, Jesus was also sold for a pittance of silver by his brothers, falsely accused, and innocently imprisoned, yet favored and blessed by God, full of God's Spirit and wisdom, and exalted and set over His heavenly kingdom. God's image bearers are capable of unimaginable violence for the sake of the god who wields the most power in our lives, the god named "me." When we become caught in self-worship and refuse to know God, we become unrecognizable. We become image bearers who cheat, take from, afflict heavy burdens, ruthlessly oppress, kill, and cast away precious life, treating people as if they are disposable and not a precious treasure of God's. And God allows this to happen. As Romans 1:24–25 says, "Therefore God gave them up in the lusts of their hearts to impurity, to the dishonoring of their bodies among themselves, because they exchanged the truth about God for a lie and worshipped and served the creature rather than the Creator, who is blessed forever! Amen."

Joseph's story is found in the first book of the Bible, Genesis. Genesis recounts God's perfect creation and His love for mankind. In the Garden of Eden, Adam and Eve walked with God. Unity and harmony existed between God, people, and the animals. We received our purpose from Him —knowing Him as our Creator. We existed for His pleasure and delight, and we received pleasure and delight from walking with Him. God did not stifle or oppress his creation. He bestowed upon them the greatest honor, being made in His likeness. Like Pharaoh honored Joseph and entrusted him with all that he had while retaining authority over him, God gave Adam dominion over His creation. Adam only submitted to God, the King of creation. God always ruled over Adam and Eve; not even with perfect harmony between God and man have we ever been God's equal. We were meant to joyfully serve Him in submission, secure in God's favor and love. Creation was perfect, complete, and whole. We humans lacked nothing.

While this is hard for us to acknowledge and accept, our omniscient, omnipresent, and omnipotent God intentionally crafted His creation to have limitations. Some of our limitations include needs for survival, such as food, water, and sleep, limitations in what our minds can comprehend, such as in fully understanding our limitless Creator, and limitations in what our unassisted eyes can see. Whereas God sees the entirety of the miniscule to the massive simultaneously and perfectly, we need telescopes to see far into the universe and microscopes to see the minute, and rarely can we hold both cohesively. These limitations, however, do not speak to any creative imperfections on the part of God nor any nefarious intent on His part to keep us under His control. He was a parent who lovingly cares for His child, and Adam and Eve were the object of His affection. They were intentionally made to be reliant upon our Maker because it is His delight to sustain them. They were made to trust Him and to gratefully accept His provision. He looked upon them with favor. His arm stretched out towards them and upheld them, and it never grew weary or tiresome for Him. They walked with Him and communed with Him. They looked upon His face because His face was ever turned towards them, but at no time did they gaze upon His face in equality. God lovingly provided for and lovingly delegated.

God, however, did not demand their submission. He offered His creation a choice. Genesis 2:16 tells us, "And the LORD God commanded the man, saying, 'You may surely eat of every tree of the garden, but of the tree of the knowledge of good and evil you shall not eat, for in the day that you eat of it you shall surely die." Satan provided just enough doubt in Eve's heart to encourage her to defy God's orders, and the Fall of all mankind came when Adam and Eve did not submit to God's authority, choosing themselves over God. Genesis 3:6 summarizes this event: "So, when the woman saw that the tree was good for food, and that it was a delight to the eyes, and that the tree was to be desired to make one wise, she took of its fruit and ate, and she also gave some to her husband who was with her, and he ate." This decision had catastrophic consequences that began with a loss of intimacy with God. Never had they hid themselves from God, but now the recognition of sin causes a divide in their relationship with Him, and humanity has been hiding from God ever since.

Defiance, wickedness, and shame are born in an instant that does not end with Adam and Eve. Tragically, Eve was not alone in her quest for equality with God. The Fall moves forward into the hearts of every human being, making our current state contrary to how we were designed. We were made to worship God and to commune with Him. What happens when, like Eve, we want our knowledge to be equal or exceed that of God? What happens when our knowledge, which should leave no doubt of the supremacy of our Creator God, concludes that God does not exist, that we can manage things without Him, that He is irrelevant, or that He is too close-minded to accept us, so instead, we refuse Him? What happens when we are so obstinately rooted and grounded in our own course of action that we refuse to yield like Pharaoh? If we reject the knowledge of God long enough, God hands us over to our desires and eventually we become blind to the truth. Our knowledge problem worsens and worsens until God completely disappears from our view and, in our minds, ceases to exist.

Like this Pharaoh of old, we are all born with a knowledge problem. We are unable to see God in His fullness, power, holiness, and goodness. We are unable to see ourselves in our true state. We want to hold onto the belief that humanity is mostly good, that we are not fallen and sinful, and that we have the right to decide what is just and tolerable. We want to be kings of our own lives, able to determine who we are and what we were made for, but sin is a deceitful trap that turns us, in our longing for kingly rule, into slaves obeying our own desire for the quest for sin that never satisfies. Sin is a prison wrapped in lavish, enticing promises that keep us imprisoned until there is no way out. Lovingly, God warns us that any innate goodness in humanity was separated from us when sin drove a divide between us and the source of all goodness. Psalm 51:5 gives us that warning this way, "Behold, I was brought forth in iniquity, and in sin did my mother conceive me." Oh, how difficult it is for us to accept this truth. But this truth is not meant to condemn us, keep us in a place of shame, or diminish our value but to show us a greater value, value that came at the cost of Jesus's life. Truth warns and drives awareness that there is another way, a better way available to each of us, born from grace, mercy, and love. If we just turn from our pride, we can enter an unshakeable, life-changing covenant. But what God reveals as truth and what we long to be true are conflicting ideas. Each of us must make a choice: either choose God and deny ourselves or choose ourselves and deny God. No matter how hard we try to make both fit together, we cannot have both and live.

Justice is symbolized with scales because it involves weighing the evidence of two sides in fairness. It consists of seeking out truth and weighing the motives of one's heart to lovingly defend and restore the wronged party. But simply determining fault stops short of true justice.

Justice requires judgment to make a wrong situation right again. Otherwise, we would only have an acknowledgement of the truth without accountability. The roots of weighing two objects against each other originate in Egypt and are recorded in the Book of the Dead. To determine a right and just heart, the heart of the dead was weighed against a feather. A heart the weight of a feather was granted favor, and paradise was the person's everlasting resting place. A heart heavier than a feather was consumed by one of their gods. This indicates that, even if we do not follow God, we inherently understand the heaviness of sin, a weight we cannot bear. But with God that weariness goes away, and we soar on wings like eagles, our hearts lighter than a feather, able to withstand judgment. That image comes from Isaiah 40:31: "but they who wait for the LORD shall renew their strength; they shall mount up with wings like eagles; they shall run and not be weary; they shall walk and not faint."

Just as scales need to be calibrated periodically for accuracy, to make sure they properly weigh items, our perception of justice also needs to be calibrated. We are skewed in how we view the weight of our sin in comparison to God. God is the only one with a perfect view of what is just and good, whereas we tend to define goodness in comparison to one another and based on what we can see. In truth, we *all* have a desperate need of the righteousness of Jesus. In our justice, we view circumstances upside down. We inaccurately view ourselves on a very high plain, neither low nor wallowing in a pit, and we view God as dead and buried.

Somehow, we are confused about who is on trial. The Bible reveals to us that we will all stand in judgment, where God will one day weigh the heaviness of our hearts. Each of us will give an account of ourselves before God. But, instead of seeking to understand how to be able to stand in judgment before Almighty God and avoid being consumed, we instead put God on trial. We compare our actions to God's consequences; we cry injustice, cruelty, and intolerance, so we reject Him. Taking in the act alone, we think eternal death seems a very steep price to pay for eating a piece of fruit. As the right and true Judge, God does not need to defend Himself. He is not the one on trial. Yet we continually question His goodness and the motives of God's heart as if He were. When comparing His rules to our actions, we incorrectly weigh the evidence and convict Him. Our actions are an indication of the rejection of God's ways, His headship, and His provision. It is the heart behind the action that is the downfall of man. It is not our actions alone that condemn us but our defiant hearts, which lead us to act defiantly. Just as Adam and Eve discovered, weighed against the goodness of God's heart, our heavy hearts betray our guilt.

Our hearts are heavy indeed, unable to stand up against the featherweight of God's uprightness. We drastically miss the mark of His righteousness and perfection. Romans 1:22–25 describes both what we have done and how God punishes us: "Claiming to be wise, they became fools, and exchanged the glory of the immortal God for images resembling mortal man and birds and animals and creeping things. Therefore God gave them up in the lusts of their hearts to impurity, to the dishonoring of the bodies among themselves, because they exchanged the truth about God for a lie and worshiped and serve the creature rather than the Creator, who is blessed forever! Amen." We challenged God's rightful place of honor and power, and we did not become like God. We untethered ourselves from the mighty, loving arm securely holding us and we fell into a pit, bearing the weight of the consequence of our choice. We have rejected the glory of God. We have compared ourselves to His glory and find Him lacking and find ourselves superior. We walk to completion the path of our choosing and blame Him for the consequences. As Romans 3:23 summarizes, "For all have sinned and fall short of the glory of God."

In Matthew 15:14, Jesus gives a warning about the Pharisees: "Let them alone; they are blind guides. And if the blind lead the blind, both will fall into a pit." All of humanity is similar. Bearing the weight of our own defiant hearts, we have become frail and broken. We cannot see our upcoming demise. The dark pit which we are trapped in provides sanctuary for our pride and our right to choose, so we confuse a dark, ensnaring trap for freedom and light. We become slaves to our lies and our own sin. In John 3:20, Jesus warns, "For everyone who does wicked things hates the light and does not come to the light, lest his works should be exposed." These terrifying, seemingly severe verses are a loving warning to turn from our ways to be rescued. The day is coming when we will *all* be humbled. Isaiah 2:10–12 gives us a warning about that day, "Enter into the rock and hide in the dust from before the terror of the Lord, and from the splendor of his majesty. The haughty looks of man shall be brought low, and the lofty pride of men shall be humbled, and the Lord alone will be exalted in that day. For the LORD of hosts has a day against all that is proud and lofty, against all that is lifted up—and it shall be brought low."

This story in Exodus shows the position and actions of kings and slaves, both indicative of the false identities we hold. Both identities highlight the depths of our knowledge problem and speak to the defiance and shame that were born when sin entered the world. They represent opposite ends of the spectrum of worth, from the most exalted to the lowliest. The antonyms of the word *King* are *minion*, *underling*, and *subordinate*. The opposite of *kingly* is *lowly*. But what makes a minion, an underling, or a subordinate even more lowly? Force. Being forced to be one, a slave. How fitting it is that God introduces knowledge of His dominion over all the earth, including mankind, by displaying His deliverance amongst this spectrum of exalted kings and lowly slaves. Too often, we view ourselves from one of these extremes. In defiance, we think of ourselves as kings in control of our domain, the gods we were set on this earth to please, when we are slaves to sin in disguise. Or we recognize that we control nothing, and instead of embracing God's act of deliverance and His adoption of us, we dwell in shame and wallow in our slavery. Romans 8:15 describes what God has done this way, "For you did not receive the spirit of slavery to fall back into fear, but you have received the Spirit of adoption as sons, by whom we cry, 'Abba! Father!'"

All too often we look at self-exalting pride as a cliff with a sheer drop-off into the abyss. Wanting to avoid falling off, we move further and further from the edge, but there is a counterpart to self-exalting pride known as self-effacing pride, a pride that is masked to look like humility. Not realizing the self-effacing arm of pride has a cliff and drop-off of its own, we draw precariously close to the edge. Neither of these identities is the identity that God intends for us. Our pride and rebellion grasps at making ourselves kings, causing us to defy God's rule and reject His reign, when there is only one King. If we believe we are nothing, we tend to live as if we are nothing. As slaves, our self-doubt hides that we are really doubting the healing power of God, the King in our lives, so we pursue our sins of the past, stuck in shame with the recognition that we are not worthy of the exaltation that God has brought to our lives. Yet, it is the sacrifice of Jesus which defines our worth. But being slaves to sin is not where we remain, because God sent a rescuer to deliver us from our slavery. He calls us His own and He dwells in our midst. He made us co-heirs to His kingdom. In Romans 8:16–17, Paul describes this reality and how we know it: "The Spirit himself bears witness with our spirit that we are children of God, and if children, then heirs— heirs of God and fellow heirs with Christ, provided we suffer with him in order that we may also be glorified with him."

We look at some people, and we see that they seem to have it all. They have avoided the hardships and pitfalls that plague most of us. We label them *fortunate*, but God has taught me otherwise. What if *easy*, *empowered*, and *comfortable* are the most dangerous positions to find ourselves in? What if having it all causes us to view ourselves as "god"- kings? What if it puffs up our hearts to such a level of hardness that it eliminates our ability to see the truth of God? The entire lives of the people who have it all are built on their own lofty places. The prophet Obadiah declared in Obadiah 1:3, concerning the people of Edom, "The pride of your heart has deceived you, you who live in the clefts of the rock, in your lofty dwelling, who say in your heart, 'Who will bring me down to the ground?'" What do those who have it all need of God? But one day, they will be brought low. Obadiah warned Edom in Obadiah 1:4, "Though you soar aloft like the eagle, though your nest is set among the stars, from there I will bring you down, declares the LORD." Imagine, the difficulty it would take to yield to God, when you live like a king? Even with a rough, bumpy road, we can so easily fall into the mentality that we are kings in control, when we are nothing but slaves posing as kings. Recently, I had a conversation with a friend who talked about the brokenness that God has brought into his life. He talked about how, looking back, he saw God giving him opportunity after opportunity to turn from his previous behaviors, but he did not stop to listen or take the time to see until everything was taken away from him and he found himself at the point of brokenness. Finally, he was able to see that he was in a pit all along. Now, he finds himself in a place of gratitude for the brokenness. When we finally arrive at this place of laying down our pride crown, we no longer toil. We find contentment as we sense God lifting us out of the pit.

David corrects our perspective in Psalm 8:1 when he writes, "O LORD, our Lord, how majestic is your name in all the earth! You have set your glory above the heavens." As much as our sight is tainted by an elevated view of our own importance, such a view equally skews the majesty and elevation of God, downgrading God to the level of mankind. He alone is the King of Kings. The scale of purity, holiness, majesty, and glory which compares God with mankind is perfectly unbalanced. God's glorious righteousness and majesty reaches up to the heavens to the same degree that we, in our own righteousness, are trapped in the pit. We are not all-knowing nor all-powerful, yet we maneuver as if we are. We are meant to live in full reliance on God, but, in our defiance, we move in wrath and folly, railing against this truth. In contrast, God sees all things clearly and without the need of any tools or instruments. Yet we challenge Him as if we are His equal. David recognized our true status in Psalm 8:4–6, "What is man that you are mindful of him, and the son of man that you care for him? Yet you have made him a little lower than the heavenly beings and crowned him with glory and honor. You have given him dominion over the works of your hands; you have put all things under his feet."

What do we need to understand about our knowledge problem? It has impaired our ability to see clearly. Creation is groaning and God's perfection has been eroded because of sin. Entropy has occurred. Our sight, both spiritually and physically, has worsened. Now, glasses are commonplace for many of us in everyday life to see normal-sized objects. Our sight without them is like the unfocused lens of a microscope. The first task of our morning consists of grasping blindly for glasses to help us see what creation, in its perfection, had readily made available to us. Likewise, spiritually, our days consist of spiritually grasping at blurred identities, hoping to satisfy the void inside.

I distinctly remember my biology days and the effort it took to focus the microscope to the precise level needed to see the object under the glass clearly. What I remember so distinctly was the frustration of not knowing whether I needed to dial in closer or move the lens further away or whether the specimen glass itself needed to be moved. There were times I thought we would never get a clear image. So, once an object became somewhat clear, I would want to quickly remove my hand from the knob and not *ever* touch it again. If your lab partner wanted to "make it better" and turned the knob, you wanted to scream, "*No*! Why did you touch it? Leave it alone. It was good!" It is like Eve took God's microscope and turned the knob with a resounding "*crank*!" His microscope, which was perfectly dialed in for the purposes of His created beings, was satisfying, restful, and good, but instead of being joyful with the detailed view God had shared with her, she attempted to make everything clearer for herself. And instead of enhanced sight, everything became distorted and blurry. Uh-oh! Now, no matter how hard we try, we cannot get it dialed back in again. So, rather than admit our blindness and seek help to correct it, we deemed blurriness normal. Now, our knowledge problem has expanded due to outright defiance. We substitute sight for blindness and blindness for sight.

Oh, how quickly we see humanity fall farther and farther away from the knowledge of truth as Adam and Eve blame instead of confessing, driving a wedge not only between themselves and God but also a wedge between one another! We see sin gain traction as defiance and disunity quickly move to violence, evidenced by the actions of Cain. Instead of submitting to God and doing right, his anger toward God is unleashed on his brother. His hatred of humility supersedes all love and care for his own brother and murder is born. Throughout the remainder of Genesis, mankind continues to do evil in God's sight and only a few sporadically submit to God's ways. We see the recording of the perpetuation of despicable acts that man commits against God and against one another. We see humanity give themselves over to their pride and their flesh, blinded to the reality that they bear the image of the living God, losing the knowledge of their true calling and purpose. We lose the -understanding of our true selves, no longer considering what we were created for. We live for ourselves when we were created to live for God. We create our own identity instead of living the identity God created us for. Nothing continually and fully satisfies us, because we have rejected the only One who can satisfy the longing inside of us. We become relentless in our grasping, in our toiling, and in our trying to define our value and our worth and to assuage the emptiness that we feel, no matter the cost to those around us. In our grasping for happiness, satisfaction, and power, we have become hard and selfish, and we have lost sight of one another. We see our brothers and our sisters as our enemies. We take advantage of others to better serve ourselves. We wage war. We oppress the weak. God puts our condition under the microscope and sees with perfect focus, delivering His verdict in Isaiah 48:22: "'There is no peace,' says the Lord, 'For the wicked'."

As we move along in Genesis, wickedness becomes so severe that God destroys humankind in a flood. Genesis 6:5-7 tells us that "The Lord saw that the wickedness of man was great in the earth, and that every intention of the thoughts of his heart was only evil continually. And the LORD regretted that he had made man on the earth, and it grieved him to his heart. So the LORD said, 'I will blot out man whom I have created from the face of the land, man and animals and creeping things and birds of the heavens, for I am sorry that I have made them." As the story of mankind's choices continues, the hope of redemption appears to dim. Except in God's mercy and grace, He spares one family, Noah's family, and we discover the comingling of God's justice with His mercy. Knowing that it would be just a matter of time before our wickedness returned to this degree, rather than leaving us in our hopeless state, God continually intervenes, and He provides a glimmer of hope by approaching one man, Abraham, and making a covenant with him. God promises him a family and through this family, Joseph's family, God's mercy and grace will save the world.

It is with pleasure that I dig into the book of Exodus. A book so familiar from my childhood, yet, now with new eyes and a softer heart, so refreshingly new. I remember hearing these fantastic stories of God bringing low the Egyptians, and what stuck with me for all those years were the mighty plagues and the death of the Egyptians for their disobedience. If you would have asked me to describe the God revealed in the book of Exodus and Numbers, I would have told you, "smoke and fire. The one who gives laws and sets the world on notice of who the real God is. A God who expects His people to *perfectly* obey Him." The nugget of truth taken with me from this book was "do not mess with God." "Be obedient! Follow the rules!If you want to live, remember the importance of being on God's side." My impression was that God seemed way more vengeful and destructive than merciful. I saw severe consequences that could not be reversed, plagues, the death of His own people, and the destruction of entire nations. Where were the mercy and grace that God speaks of?

The God I now see is a kind, gentle, loving, and patient God who knows and makes Himself known to both His own people and to the Egyptians. He makes Himself known to Moses, the prince of Egypt, and to the most insignificant Israelite slave. It is so easy to focus on the harsh moments and misunderstand the very nature of our God. I have come to realize that my view of God's wrath had more to do with my own heart of rebellion, a higher view of my own goodness that rebelled against God's justice than my view of God's justice itself, than having a true picture of God. God's judgment upon Egypt was a consequence after four hundred years of oppression, not a random, rash act on the part of God. In between reading about God claiming that He will harden the heart of Pharaoh and killing the firstborn in all the land of Egypt, I missed the abounding examples of His loving words and actions, because I was focused on the examples of His wrath. It caused me to draw an incomplete conclusion. I saw a mighty and powerful, yet unyielding and unmerciful God. Now, as I reread this story, I see example after example of God's love, His mercy, and His grace intermingled with His judgment. The acts committed against the Israelites were heinous and committed for no other reason than that the Israelites had God's favor, and that favor drove fear into the heart of Pharaoh. As I Imagine my life being made bitter with harsh slavery or my son being carelessly thrown in a river, I imagine that I would cry out to God for not only deliverance but also for justice, for Him to come and set right the senseless suffering inflicted upon me and to punish the one who had so little regard for me and those that I love.

One night, my study group was discussing Genesis 22 and the difficulty of deciding, in faith, to willingly sacrifice your own son. "After these things God tested Abraham and said to him, "Abraham!" And he said, "Here I am." He said, "Take your son, your only son Isaac, whom you love, and go to the land of Moriah, and offer him there as a burnt offering on one of the mountains of which I shall tell you.'" (Genesis 22:1–2 ESV). Despite this extraordinarily hard request, nothing in the remaining passage indicates the slightest hesitation on the part of Abraham to complete God's request. Wow, what an ask. Our first thoughts are naturally centered on the severity of God's request. *Why would a God who claims to be good and who promises life and blessing make such a request? Would my faith hold strong against such a request? Would my faith hold strong in the face of a fraction of this request?* What a hard situation to take in. Our minds tend to view this story as horrific, as a case of child abuse and a barely escaped murder, when the point is to see the beauty of holding nothing back from God, even what you love most, because He is that trustworthy. Everything we possess has been entrusted to us by God. He held nothing back, even what He loved most, for us. Abraham understood that this life is a shadow of the promise to come. Hebrews 11:13–16 tells us about this understanding: "These all died in faith, not having received the things promised, but having seen them and greeted them from afar, and having acknowledged that they were strangers and exiles on the earth. For people who speak thus make it clear that they are seeking a homeland. If they had been thinking of that land from which they had gone out, they would have had opportunity to return. But as it is, they desire a better country, that is, a heavenly one. Therefore, God is not ashamed to be called their God, for he has prepared for them a city."

Another story that similarly stirs something within me is the story of Moses's birth. "The woman conceived and bore a son, and when she saw that he was a fine child, she hid him three months. When she could hide him no longer, she took for him a basket made of bulrushes and daubed it with bitumen and pitch. She put the child in it and placed it among the reeds by the river bank." (Exodus 2:2–3). As I consider Jochebed, the mother of Moses, I realize that she was a woman who trusted God, a woman who waited on His deliverance, but who likely died a slave in a foreign land. We do not hear of her at all in the wilderness. Why would God allow someone who defied what was wrong and stood for what was right to suffer in so many ways and never witness His deliverance? Sure, God rescued Moses from death, but Jochebed lost her claim on her son as he became someone else's son. As a mother, my heart cries out against that in every way. From only my human, angry vantage point, I most certainly could view God as uncaring, cruel, or unfair. *How could you do this to someone who loves You and trusts You?* For a time that was exactly my heart. I would think, *God, I will trust you with my salvation, but I won't give you my life because I know You ask for everything and You take too much!* But I have come to know God through my own brokenness, hardship, and pain. I have discovered that God *is* worth it. I have come to know a God who uses pain and hardship, not from cruelty but to make Himself known to us. I have come to know this God who works in these horrible moments to bring me life. I've experienced an abundance that is not determined by earthly circumstances or earthly gain. This moment in Jochebed's life brought salvation to her people. We all will be forced to answer the question, Is it worth laying down my life to further God's plan? We can so easily fall into the mentality that we are kings, who deserve cushy, happy, and easy lives, when what we grasp to give us those lives enslaves us to the evil powers beyond our authority.

As I read of this mother risking her family to protect her son for three months and then finding herself out of options, I feel for her. Could you even imagine laying him down in the basket and placing him in the water? Did God speak to her and promise her a good outcome, or did she have to rely solely on hope and faith? Unlike Abraham, who knew Isaac was the promised son who had not completed his purpose, there were no promises given to her (that we are aware of) about Moses. I am not trying to minimize the significance of Abraham's moment of faith; it was a big ask and a big step in obedience, but at least there was a promise that Abraham could hold on to; God's blessing was to come through Isaac, so somehow God would ensure Isaac lived. Abraham had experienced the steady and true nature of God's promises despite impossible circumstances, so he walked without wavering, knowing God's promises never waiver. Did Jochebed experience the steady and true nature of God's promises in her life as well? I wonder if this mother was left questioning if it was in God's will for Him to intervene? Did she question whether this child, that she lovingly cared for, would bring glory to God through his death instead of by his deliverance? With no options left, she had no choice but to let go because his rescue was in her relinquishment of him. Maybe this story hits me harder because of my season of life. Two children have grown, another child is a couple of years away from adulthood, and I am learning to come to terms with laying them down, not knowing what the hardships of life will bring them, not able to insulate them from the dangers of the world any longer.

Then it struck me. All the actions of Jochebed speak of a faith that did not need to *see* God's deliverance to live and thrive. So often, we feel like we need to see it, to see something, anything that indicates God's movement of bringing bad to good. What might be holding you back today? What are you waiting for God to make right before you move in faith, when your movement might just be the very thing that He uses to move His kingdom forward? Because of her faith, Jochebed was able to truly see God. She had a better look at God's deliverance than most of the Israelites who physically witnessed it as they crossed the Red Sea on dry land.

I so badly want to see my children walk in the truth with a tenacity and a fervor that matches how much God loves them, because they understand the depths to which they are loved. My desire for them would be to avoid the heartaches and the brokenness that walking away from God wrought in my life. How difficult it has been for me to accept that their faith and their walk must be their own! I cannot create it for them. How difficult it has been for me to realize that I am being asked to truly let go of the control that I falsely think I yield to God. I feel as if I am in the position of Jochebed, lovingly protecting my children for as long as I am able. Now, it is time to let go and wait on deliverance, praying that God draws them from the water and provides them with a holy purpose and that they do not succumb to the watery, life-robbing depths of the world. Am I OK with any outcome, knowing that His glory might require hard and painful things? *Will I still retain my belief in your goodness, God, if I watch them struggle or pursue the world over You? Do I trust You enough to watch the rescue from the relinquishment of the lives of my children?*

Then, I realize that, like Abraham, we have all received promises from God, and they fill my soul with peace and acceptance. God loves all my children more than I do. He is more faithful than I could ever hope to be. God is a relentlessly pursuing, personal God who calls, heals, and transforms. He does not let any of His own be snatched away. *You promise that nothing happens that You do not turn to good for those who love You and are called according to Your purpose. Lord, I confess I cannot do it. I cannot make any of my children understand their value in You or make them love You with all that is in them, no matter how much I wish it. I can model your heart. I can testify to your goodness, but You, alone, call hearts and bring deliverance. I pray to You today. Prepare me to lay each one down when the time comes and, in faith, to wait expectantly for Your deliverance. Protect my children during their time in the water, when they are no longer in the safety of my arms and they are vulnerable and exposed to the dangers of the world around them. Bring them a rescuer to draw them out. Let them see Your face. Solidify their purposes and their prosperity in You. Let them know You. Help them to vulnerably share their desires and their fears with You and teach them that they are known and called by name. Send them out into the world to testify about You and make You known.*

PAUSE TO PRAISE AND PONDER:

Exodus begins with the exalted and the lowly. Pharaoh leads his people down a wicked path, and the Israelites bear his mistreatment.
Read Exodus 1:8–14.

Theme: We tend to view ourselves improperly as kings or slaves.

Praise: Read Exodus 2:23–25. How have you experienced our God who hears our cries, remembers us, and knows us?

Brainstorming: What makes you feel like a king?

- What are your expectations?
- What makes you have a bad day?

What do you feel enslaved by?

- What do you hide?
- What drains you?
- What makes you feel overwhelmed, anxious, or exhausted?

Mirror: God used the story of the Israelites to show the world that He is a God who delivers His people from slavery. He also shows that He is a God who has a plan that follows a path that might not look like the path we would choose.
How is God using your story to show His nature of love and deliverance to the world?
- Reflect on your hardships.
- Reflect on your open doors and unique opportunities.
Ask God to reveal to you how He will use these hardships and open doors for His glory. What fears and failures from your past are holding you back from stepping toward what God has in store for you?

Get Creative:
- Draw a throne and write, in the space underneath the throne, the areas of your life you need to lay at the feet of Jesus.
- Draw a broken chain. Write the enslaving things in your life within the broken link of the chain. Take a moment to remember that Jesus has freed us from all shame and condemnation.

Daily Bread: In what ways can you bring God praise? How is He greater than mankind and how does He extend favor to mankind?

- Draw a drinking glass. Select a verse that speaks the truth about the ways and promises of God. Make sure it is related to what God has revealed to you today as you pondered.
- Draw a sandwich. On the bottom bun, praise God by writing what you know of His splendor and majesty.
    - Select an aspect of your story that God revealed to you as you pondered that you need to hand over to Him and write it in the meat portion of the sandwich.
    - Consider both how you have come to know God and what He reveals about Himself in the Bible. Continue to praise God by answering how God is fully able to free you and why should we revere Him. Write these answers on the top bun of the sandwich.

3

I AM

Exodus 3:14, "*God said to Moses, 'I AM WHO I AM.' And he said, 'Say this to the people of Israel: 'I AM has sent me to you.'"*

I watch true crime because I am fascinated by how a detective works to follow the clues to find the perpetrator to bring justice for the victim. Forensic tools that leave little doubt of guilt have been developed through advancements in science. Instruments specifically designed to help people gain insight into what is not visible to the naked eye, such as the presence of blood, the pattern of fingerprints, and unique DNA markers, are used to give police evidence for a specific conclusion about the crime by allowing them to place suspects at the crime scene. Sometimes, however, detectives can miss clues and forgo leads, blinded by their own beliefs about the identity of the culprit. Instead of leading them to follow the clues and evidence left at the crime scene, their own skewed perception causes them to miss the truth.

Psalm 19:1–4 declares, "The heavens declare the glory of God, and the sky above proclaims his handiwork. Day to day pours out speech, and night to night reveals knowledge. There is no speech, nor are there words, whose voice is not heard. Their voice goes out through all the earth, and their words to the end of the world. In them he has set a tent for the sun." Like detectives, if we follow the clues of creation, we are led to a Creator God. Day and night His creation speaks of Him. Evidence for God is all over His creation, and we can look at it the way that detectives look at fingerprints and DNA. However, like Pharaoh, our hard-heartedness prevents the recognition of the truth. Exodus 8:19 (NIV) records the Pharaoh's problem: "The magicians said to Pharaoh, 'This is the finger of God.' But Pharaoh's heart was hard and he would not listen, just as the LORD had said." The very things that speak to the identity of the crime's perpetrator, due to his uniqueness, speak to the design of the Creator Who uniquely crafted him.

We cannot understand how truly blind we are, if we do not first understand that we are blind. Creation provides that knowledge to us. The proof of His creation leads us to understand that there is a Creator. Based on only the works of God's hands, humanity's blindness towards Him is without excuse. Romans 1:19–20 tells us, "For what can be known about God is plain to them, because God has shown it to them. For his invisible attributes, namely, his eternal power and divine nature, have been clearly perceived, ever since the creation of the world, in the things that have been made. So they are without excuse." Life itself, the unique structure of every living thing, and the self-sustaining nature of creation all speak to a Master Creator of detailed precision. God, Himself, laid the foundations of the earth and the heavens are the work of His hands (Hebrews 1:10). God's vastness is on display through His universe, His depths are on display through His oceans, and His precision is on display through the self-sustaining balance of plants and animals. His detailed work is on display through individual defining DNA and fingerprints. God's own fingerprints are all over creation, pointing to Him as the Designer. Even with a blurred microscope God has made a way for us to glimpse the outline of a Master Creator. Unfortunately, simply having the knowledge that a creator God exists does not automatically rescue us from the pit, but it does reveal to us that there is Someone mightier than us, bringing us a step closer to the full recognition of our blindness. We are scared, naked, and hopeless and cannot get out of the pit without intervention. But graciously, God does not leave us in our hopeless state, not able to know Him. Like the Sower who scatters seed plentifully in the Parable of the Sower, God generously makes himself known to all who will hear and listen (Mark 4:3–20). Since the time that God shed blood to clothe Adam and Eve in animal skins (Genesis 3:21), thereby instituting the temporary peace offering repeated in the Law of Moses (Leviticus 3), God has been working out His plan of rescue and redemption through His permanent peace offering, the blood of Jesus. The entire Old Testament is the buildup of God's revelation of rescue through His Son, Jesus Christ. The entire New Testament is the explanation of the good news of Jesus and His promised gift of salvation through grace and how He is the revelation and fulfillment of the Old Testament. As the history of the nation of Israel was unfolding, God used countless lives to reveal His plan of rescue to the world. He worked in the hearts of His treasured nation to craft His love letter to us all: a letter written over thousands of years, collected, and named the Bible. This letter contains God's very words and breathes life into its hearers today.

The Bible, often viewed as a stale, outdated, black-and-white set of rigid rules, is bursting with vibrant color and life. It is awesome! Majestic! Life-giving! Through it, we find a kaleidoscope of ways to discover and know God, a myriad of fascinating combinations that, if we took the time to ponder, to ask, seek, and knock, we could see with a precision that the human eye cannot. God has given us a different type of microscope, not one that we see with our eyes but one that gives sight through our ears. While creation is the display of God's existence, we are introduced to God Himself through hearing, and it is by hearing that we come to know him. As Romans 10:17 says, "So faith comes from hearing, and hearing through the word of Christ."

Through His Word, we discover that God's sight is unparalleled. It is completely unbound. He can see the fullness and entirety of His creation while also having sight to uniquely etch our fingerprints and knit together our DNA. It is impossible for me, a constrained being, to grasp the vastness of the infinite and the eternal. I stretch my brain to try and comprehend the highest number imaginable, and then I keep adding one, until it boggles my mind. Our bound minds can only vaguely grasp the concept of limitlessness, but we cannot fully comprehend it. Yet, ironically, while I do not completely understand it, my heart longs for it. As Solomon, the wisest man who ever lived, said in Ecclesiastes 3:11, "He has made everything beautiful in its time. Also, he has put eternity into man's heart, yet so that he cannot find out what God has done from the beginning to the end."

Infinity and eternity convey the boundless aspects of our boundless God. As creatures of limitation, we should see God's creation and know His supremacy. We should understand that there is someone greater than us to look toward and to worship, and we should recognize that there is a God so mighty that we cannot compare, nor can we touch Him without His intervention.

The Bible is full of history, poetry, hyperbole, prophecy, warning, and instruction. It teaches us about God through the testimony of others: their history, their description of His ways and His heart, their worship and praise of His goodness, and their testimony of what they have witnessed and heard. It contains the history of God's people, God's intervention and rescue of their lives, and God's holy and righteous laws and decrees. Through it, we learn that God came down and walked with us because He chose to make a way for us. He rescued not because our goodness compelled Him but simply because His favor rests upon us. We learn that Adam and Eve's community with Him, their authentic, intimate relationship, occurred only because He upheld them in His hand.

When man fell, God came down to rescue us so He could walk with us once more. It is only through this belief in God's rescue, through the sacrifice of Jesus on the cross, that we can know God. Colossians 1:19–20 speaks of who Jesus was and how he came to rescue us: "For in him all the fullness of God was pleased to dwell, and through him to reconcile to himself all things, whether on earth or in heaven, making peace by the blood of his cross." Until we understand the level to which we have fallen, how we have rejected Him and put Him on trial, we cannot fully appreciate His act of rescue. John 1:9–12 tells us, "The true light, which gives light to everyone, was coming into the world. He was in the world, and the world was made through him, yet the world did not know him. He came to his own, and his own people did not receive him. But to all who did receive him, who believed in his name, he gave the right to become children of God." And gloriously, somewhere in the middle of learning all about this God through the eyes and ears of His followers, as they face challenges and insurmountable odds and find rest and victory by putting their trust in Him, we personally meet Him ourselves. God's microscope of holy, precious things that have been hidden and were lost is finally found. It is waiting to be discovered, but it requires seeking it and laying aside our sight as we know it. It requires humility, patience, daring to ask, and then waiting for the promise of blessed sight.

The Bible conveys the marvelous nature of God through His names, His words, His works, and His ways. His names reveal His character and holiness. His words, His works, and His ways provide a harmonious trio working together to make God known to us. These attributes of God form a collective whole displaying the very character and radiant glory of God. The book of Exodus is a wonderful example of these harmonious revelations. Exodus is an exciting, action-packed story containing God's rescue of His people. Deliverance through the mighty I Am is as relevant and holds as true for our enslaved lives today as it was for the Israelite slaves. God's words speak of His wondrous promises to rescue His people and His desire to provide for them. God's works display His mighty deeds of deliverance. They leave no room for doubt that He is the Lord God Almighty, who stands above all other gods. His sovereignty, majesty, and might are on display throughout the entire narrative. We discover that nothing can stop the plans of God, not His enemies, not our enemies, not even His "inadequate-for-the-task-at-hand" followers. We learn that God can restore and transform any heart, no matter how frail or wicked. God's ways display His trustworthiness, His faithfulness, and His never-ending mercy, and His gentle and lowly spirit teaches us how nothing can separate us from His love (Romans 8:38–39).

The book of Exodus begins with the names of the members of Jacob's immediate household that came into the land of Egypt. What a personal indication that these are known and remembered people, special to God! Instead of abounding favor for this group of people, as was the situation at the end of Genesis and as we would expect of God's children, we get a glimpse of a change in their position. Ever so subtly we are introduced to the precarious position of death through the death of Joseph. Exodus 1:6 tells us, "Then Joseph died, and all his brothers and all that generation." We discover that the favor of God's people has eroded with the passage of time. The leader of Egypt forgets all about Joseph and what he did for their nation, and he turns his sights on oppressing God's people. The first chapter of Exodus is riddled with the harsh atrocities that they experienced at the hands of the Egyptians. God allows it for a time, but He does not permanently stay hidden and immovable. By the end of the second chapter,

God reveals that He is not withdrawn but moving with the slightest of nuances, by the introduction of a second death. Despite how things appear, the precarious position of death now rests on the people of Egypt. Exodus 2:23–25 tells us, "During those many days the king of Egypt died, and the people of Israel groaned because of their slavery and cried out for help. Their cry for rescue from slavery came up to God. And God heard their groaning, and God remembered his covenant with Abraham, with Isaac, and with Jacob. God saw the people of Israel—and God knew." We see the house of the Lord rising even as circumstances look bleak, and, just like the good news of Jesus, the second time death comes around, it is surrounded by hope. Now, we see not a forgotten people but a people remembered, and known, by God.

After many years of silence, and year after year of slavery, God bursts forth by revealing himself to Moses in a most unusual and spectacular way. God reveals Himself through a burning bush that is not consumed by the flame. Exodus 3:2–4 says, "And the angel of the LORD appeared to him in a flame of fire out of the midst of a bush. He looked and behold, the bush was burning, yet it was not consumed. And Moses said, 'I will turn aside to see this great sight, why the bush is not burned.' When the LORD saw that he turned aside to see, God called to him out of the bush, 'Moses, Moses!' and he said, 'Here I am.'" In this conversation, we discover amazing things about God. Not only does God reveal that He sees the affliction of His people but He also reveals that He hears their cries, and we discover that God cares enough about them to come down and rescue them. Additionally, we learn that the purpose of this revelation is not only to rescue His people but also, through this rescue mission, to make himself known to Moses, to the Israelites, to the Egyptians, and to the world. I Am is set apart and superior to every other god. There is none like Him.

Over and over, we see God moving and acting in a manner that leaves no doubt that He is the mighty I AM. But He never acts rashly in an emotional wave of destruction and death. He displays His might with deliberation and patience, full of warning so any who wanted to could turn from their ways and be spared. We see God reveal His justice through His judgment against Egypt and their Pharaoh as He attacks their various gods. In Exodus 3:19–20, God tells Moses, "'But I know that the king of Egypt will not let you go unless compelled by a mighty hand. So I will stretch out my hand and strike Egypt with all the wonders that I will do in it; after that he will let you go.'" But God does not immediately attack Pharaoh. First, He reveals His intentions. Then, He makes a request, which Pharaoh completely disregards and retaliates against. Imagine the God of the universe making a request like this! "Afterward Moses and Aaron went and said to Pharaoh, 'Thus says the LORD, the God of Israel, 'Let my people go, that they may hold a feast to me in the wilderness.'' But Pharaoh said, 'Who is the LORD, that I should obey his voice and let Israel go? I do not know the LORD, and moreover, I will not let Israel go.' Then they said, 'The God of the Hebrews has met with us. Please let us go a three days' journey into the wilderness that we may sacrifice to the LORD our God, lest he fall upon us with pestilence or with the sword.' But the king of Egypt said to them, 'Moses and Aaron, why do you take the people away from their work? Get back to your burdens'" (Exodus 5:1–4). God's representatives approach Pharaoh with respect and humility, not with demands. It is Pharaoh who is mired in pride. We see a heart so hardened in Pharaoh that this request by Moses results in even more oppression against God's people.

God reveals His names to Moses; I AM WHO I AM, Yahweh, and the God of Abraham, of Isaac, and of Jacob. These names of God come with a covenant promise, so as He states them, the delivery of that statement is synonymous with the guarantee of favor upon this nation and a promise that they will be their own people and have their own land. But, at this point in history, we do not see the fulfillment of this promise. They are waiting with anticipation for the promise, a wait with anticipation that structures our faith. The promise goes down through the generations from Abraham, to Isaac, to Jacob, to the twelve sons of Israel, to their children's children and beyond.

God is both unlike and vastly superior to the gods of Egypt. He is unlike and vastly superior to our gods today. A huge takeaway from this book is that God knows Himself. It sounds so simple, so easy to comprehend, and not worthy of additional thought, but this is something profound to consider. When we take the time to reflect on this, to rest upon this truth, we see a foundation which we can build our lives upon. God's omnipotence, coupled with His omniscience, ensures that God's plans will be fulfilled, guaranteed, no question! He is in control, always has been in control, and always will remain in control. He will never snap, never run out of patience, and never conclude that His grace and mercy have run dry. That is not a question in His mind, ever! It is only a question in our minds. God has full confidence in His might, His victory, His character, His holiness, and His faithfulness. Unlike mankind, God does not have to move strategically to gain power. He does not have to oppress to build Himself up. He does not have to hoard anything to save it for His own use one day. God does not struggle with nor grasp at His identity. He never exhibits rash reactions. He is never surprised, never inconvenienced, never stumped, or backed into a corner, nor does He ever respond with irritability or frustration. God does not pridefully gloat; He simply reveals the truth of His glory, power, and might. It is not pride which drives Him but love. Isaiah 40:11 tells us, "He will tend his flock like a shepherd; he will gather the lambs in his arms; he will carry them in his bosom, and gently lead those that are with young."

The strong arm of the Lord is revealed to the world, displaying not only his might but also his love. In Exodus 15:11–12, Moses declares, "Who is like you, O Lord, among the gods? Who is like you, majestic in holiness, awesome in glorious deeds, doing wonders? You stretched out your right hand; the earth swallowed them." His reach can destroy His enemies. Those who do not know Him are petrified of His might. Moses describes their reaction to God in Exodus 15:16, "Terror and dread fall upon them; because of the greatness of your arm, they are still as a stone, till your people, O Lord, pass by, till the people pass by whom you have purchased." But even more amazing is that His reach is so large that He rescues and saves by pulling us from the pit.

God sees our slavery and goes to great lengths to deliver us by sending us a rescuer who willingly enters the pit with us. Through saving the Israelites, we see a God willing to stretch His arm out toward them. This unchanging God continues to stretch his arm out toward us, lifting us from the pit that we could not escape by stretching his arms wide on a cross. Isaiah 53:1 points to this reality with two questions, "Who has believed what he has heard from us? And to whom has the arm of the Lord been revealed?" His strong and mighty arm of rescue was revealed through Jesus Christ, who was despised and rejected by man. He bore our iniquity. He was smitten and afflicted by God, even though He was without sin, for us as a beautiful, precious sacrifice. God willingly laid his punishment on

Him, and Jesus has brought peace between us and God. He continues to intercede on our behalf.

In this, we find the second crucial bit of information that we need to know—God draws near to us in our slavery and oppression and makes Himself known to us. Not only does God make a way for us to be rescued, but He makes that way known to us. Jesus Christ is the way (John 14:6). God instructs us and warns us out of love. He is unrestrained in His generosity. He gives freely and lovingly. His promises do not change and are never revoked. The words that He speaks will be fulfilled and are more certain than the whole physical world around us. As Jesus said in Matthew 24:35, "Heaven and earth will pass away, but my words will not pass away." He sets the course of history in motion, working and patiently waiting for His plan to unfold. He patiently waits for us to come to know Him, for us to understand what He already knows about Himself. He endures our putting Him on trial because He is humble and loving toward us, teaching us His way of mercy and grace. He longs for us to know Him. His loving-kindness is steadfast and sure.

Exodus 3:14 records that "God said to Moses, 'I Am Who I Am.' And he said, 'Say this to the people of Israel: 'I Am has sent me to you.'" As a child I found the name I Am frustrating. In English, the verb "am" is always followed by something that describes a state of being. I wanted it to continue with an explanation. *You are what?* On its own, what does it describe? Nothing. So, on its own, what can it convey about God? As I have gotten older, I appreciate and understand its significance more and more. It not only perfectly describes the mystery, majesty, sovereignty, glory, and fullness of God, but it also describes the one attribute our God has over every other god. He is! God is, and He will always be. He lives and He brings forth life. In this simple reality, His profound, indescribable nature and the way He is the source of all life are revealed.

Amazingly, this phrase captures the essence of this God of irony that makes the last first, that makes the humble exalted, and that uses the foolishness of the world to make fools of the wise because God's folly is wiser than man's wisdom. How does one describe the unfathomable majesty, the infinite never-ending, never-beginning source of all things that we can touch, see, taste, feel, and smell? How do you explain the God who is so far above His creation, the manufacturer and producer of life, who completely focuses His love and affection towards us in mercy and grace? In the simple, the unfathomable is revealed, I AM WHO I AM!

The Hebrew word behind the name I AM is a form of the verb "haya," which means "to exist, come to pass, become, occur, abide, or remain." The word "haya" is used by Moses throughout the creation narrative in Genesis 1, in seventeen of its thirty-one verses. In Genesis, it is usually translated as "let there be" and "And there was." What we learn is that what God says, *is*. It exists. It lives. It becomes. It occurs. It remains. From creation, we learn that God is the source of order and of all things tangible. He is the God of reality. More and more, with increasing fervor and regularity, I think I AM is the most fitting name imaginable for our God. What a name to hold onto in confidence and faith when life is cruel and oppressive! What God promises, *is*! Not only is He the author of the promise but He is the fulfillment of each and every promise made. Not only did He map out His plan from before the foundation of the world but He brings each aspect of His plan to fruition. He is the wholistic Sustainer of life from beginning to end. He envisions, creates, and completes. He envisioned, created, and brought to completion the rescue of His own, and the fulfilment of all the words of God came in the form of Jesus. He is the I AM who rescued the world. John 1:1–5 tells us, "In the beginning was the Word, and the Word was with God, and the Word was God. He was in the beginning with God. All things were made through him, and without him was not any thing made that was made. In him was life, and the life was the light of men. The light shines in the darkness, and the darkness has not overcome it."

As we see with the life of Moses, when we encounter God, when He washes and sanctifies us (1 Corinthians 6:11), He changes the entire cadence and rhythm of our lives. Moses introduces the entire Torah with "Let there be" (haya) and "There was" (haya), as if it was the cadence God had placed in his heart that day. I am (haya) who I am (haya). I envision Moses writing out the creation story with a tranquil smile on his face and joy in his heart, reflecting on that day in the wilderness when God introduced himself from the bush as I AM (haya) WHO I AM (haya) and forever changed his heart. For the remainder of his days, this cadence of who God is coursed through Moses, I AM (haya) WHO I AM (haya). This knowledge of who God is propelled Moses's actions and removed his fear, I AM (haya) WHO I AM (haya). No longer was Moses focused on himself. His focus was on God, breathing in and out, I AM (haya) WHO I AM (haya). Do you recognize the cadence that God has given you?

Often, our approach is to bring the passages of God's Word in line with our viewpoints, our desires, or what is currently on our hearts and lives, and we risk distorting God to fit our desires. During one Lenten season, I wanted to be more diligent in my pursuit of being obedient to God's voice, to actively seek community with Him over absorbing Bible knowledge, and to *move* in faith, not just *voice* my faith. I decided that each day, I would actively engage in being slow to speak and being quick to listen to God. I would ask Him to reveal to me what He wanted me to hear, engaging both my heart and my mind in my Bible reading. I wanted to hear God's heart instead of simply bringing Him my wish list, concerns, fears, and desires. Ultimately, I wanted to know Him, not just know about Him. I was not looking to hide my anxious thoughts from Him but I was seeking to focus on God and His Scriptures over focusing on the anxiety in my life. I wanted to earnestly seek His wisdom over all other things in my life, even what was heavy on my heart and my mind.

What I discovered is that when I focus on God's presence, His righteousness, and His kingdom, He never ceases to answer me. And amazingly, His answer is exactly what I needed to hear to address whatever was on my heart and mind that I was attempting to lay aside. It did not eliminate the source of stress in my life, but it always gave me a greater understanding of who God is, which in turn gives me greater understanding of who I am in God. God continues to walk this out in my life and this knowledge encourages me to move in boldness and strengthens me to patiently endure in my situations. I am because *He is.* I have gone from death to life because of Him. Here are a few examples of what God, my I AM, revealed about Himself to me and how my identity and my actions fit around who He is.

The first day of seeking God's Word in this way, my heart was troubled with concern about publishing. I had finished writing a draft of my first book and had no idea what to do next. The process was overwhelming. Because I wanted to hear God speak and I wanted to hear what He wanted to say to me, I tried to suppress my anxiety and my concerns. What I discovered is that God wants us to bring Him our hearts. God met me in my anxious thoughts. At that point in the publishing process, I was trying to determine what to put in the book proposal, and it was daunting. I was filled with so much doubt about my abilities. It is so difficult to objectively analyze something that is so close to your heart. I was overwhelmed by what I did not know. I was filled with the fear of failing. I was questioning how I would ever manage to get the book published when I could not even say who the book was written for. I wrote an entire book as an outpouring of my heart with no audience in mind, or maybe more accurately, it was written for my wounded heart.

That morning, I was reading in the book of Psalms with two questions on my heart. I was asking God, *What do you want me to do in service to You today and what do you want me to learn?* Psalm 1 addresses bearing fruit and speaks of prosperity. That day, God also led me to Psalm 139:13–14, which says, "For you formed my inward parts; you knitted me together in my mother's womb. I praise you, for I am fearfully and wonderfully made. Wonderful are your works; my soul knows it very well." What amazing passages of Scripture that addressed exactly what was on my heart, my feelings of inadequacy, and potential failures. Even though I was trying to hide my fears, God spoke directly into my anxiety. He spoke about my concerns, my fears, and my desires. Within these psalms there were seeds of truth to encourage me not only through this day but through this season. Psalm 1:2–3 told me of the confidence that belongs to the person who wants to obey God: "but his delight is in the law of the LORD, and on his law he meditates day and night. He is like a tree planted by streams of water that yields its fruit in its season, and its leaf does not wither. In all that he does, he prospers," and Psalm 1:6a reminded me that "the LORD knows the way of the righteous." I was so mired down with this process, but these verses lifted the pressure and responsibility from my shoulders. I do not know the way but God does. My responsibility is to move in faith where God is guiding me because He knows the way. My role is not to fully understand or to try to control what I cannot. It was useless toil to agonize over whether the book would be accepted or successful. With joy came the understanding that I cannot fail in fulfilling the plans God has in store for me. I will bear fruit in season, if not with a published book, then in some other way. *Thank you, Lord. I will wait on You for my season to come. You know I can become easily overwhelmed and discouraged; thank You for meeting me in the concerns of my heart. Move in my heart to keep me moving forward and keep my eyes fixed on You, waiting expectantly. Prevent me from being paralyzed in fear or forging my own path. Lord, You direct my steps. Direct them now to fulfill whatever you have laid out for me. If I follow You, I will bear fruit.*

God showed me something vital about His identity that day that was skewed in my heart. God is not practically perfect or partially perfect but perfectly perfect, and this perfection includes His plan for my life even when that plan for my life comes with a severe cost to me. Every time we fear, we do not see God in His perfect perfection. His perfection is more than enough for all suffering. His perfection is more than enough for my inadequacies. He perfectly orchestrates His plan, my purpose within His plan, and His provision during the execution of His plan. I discovered a powerful truth: While I trust that His provision and His plan are perfect, I do not completely trust His path to get there. His path is often riddled with pain, brokenness, failure, and patiently waiting, so, in those moments, I question its perfection, but God uses each one of these situations and uses them for His good and ultimately for our good.

It brought me to a greater realization of my identity in relation to Him. I am a God-delighter and a God-ponderer, and with these identities comes a promise. God-delighters delight God, and God-ponderers prosper from simply loving God's ways, no special abilities needed. I am made to delight in God and to delight God with my delight of Him. This mind of mine that never stops, that has brutally attacked and imprisoned me for years, has a holy, life-giving, and non-destructive purpose. I am made to ponder God's words, His works, and His ways and to praise Him no matter what circumstances I find myself in. I am not made to scheme and seek my own quick solutions or degrade and abuse myself. If I wait on him, I will bear fruit in season. What a blessed promise!

Day two found me anxious about one of my children. My heart was heavy as only a mother seeing her child struggle understands. I tried to lay aside my worry and what was heavy on my heart to hear what God wanted to share with me. I found myself in Psalm 2 reading how the kings of the earth seek to break the bonds of the Lord. It drove me to ask God, "*Lord, how am I seeking to break the bond of needing you? How am I seeking to assume your throne? Where do I need to submit and serve you instead of demanding and seeking to rule my own life?*" The answer was in regard to my children and wanting to fix everything for them immediately. Instead of ignoring what was on my heart, just like addressing all of Moses's worries and fears, once again, God met me in the condition of my heart. My heart's cry went from *Lord, I feel helpless and overwhelmed. It is choking my joy. Please remove this from me! Heal my child!* to *Help me to hand this over to you. Teach me joy despite this situation.*

I was reminded of Joseph's words in Genesis 50:20, "As for you, you meant evil against me, but God meant it for good, to bring about that many people should be kept alive, as they are today." Oh, with joy I realized that this even applies to Satan. Even what he means as evil against my children does not remain evil against them. It was another reminder that God's path is perfect and another situation in my life where I lacked complete trust in Him. No matter the hardship, God will bring good from it to bring life to it. How precious that is to me. What a promise! *Forgive me, Lord, for not trusting Your plan with my children. Teach them to love You with all their hearts, all their souls, all their strength, and all their minds. I trust You! I trust Your plan! I trust Your path! I trust Your provision! Prevent me from praying away the neediness within my children that may be exactly what You will use to turn them fully toward You.* It was a gracious and loving reminder that God is a King who serves his servants. His cords and bonds are not oppressive and restricting but loving and safe. It was a great realization that bursting the bonds of God's dominion results in the shattering of the person. Embracing the tethering carries me safely through God's judgement. Serving in the fear of the Lord causes joy and Christ serves us as we serve Him in beautiful unity and harmony. I am made to embrace and have affection for my need, to be grateful for my dependence on God. I am not made to have disdain for or to desire to break away from Him. I rely on His refuge because I am not the ruler.

With the reminder that God is in control, that He can be trusted because His ways bless and prosper us far beyond our ways, day three found me without worry or concern. I was basking in the perfection of God. I was holding what He had shown me and was able to carry it forward beyond the day He revealed it to me. A peace and a calmness that I do not typically experience were on my heart. I am usually too busy trying to solve all my own problems instead of casting them on God. Concerns began to creep in that I would not hear specifically from God that day because I did not have a crisis to hand over to Him, and I found myself becoming anxious, questioning whether God would speak deeply and personally if I had nothing that I was anxious about. It highlighted just how bent my heart is towards anxiety that I found a way to be anxious about not being anxious. I read Psalm 3 and Jonah 1. As I quieted myself and sought His voice, I heard nothing but sensed I needed to wait on the Lord. *Yes, Lord, I will wait on You. I am waiting on You, but it would delight me today to hear your voice, for you to speak to me personally through Your Word. I want a personal, relational conversation with You every day, to talk with you as a confidante and a friend, not just when I am anxious and scared but always. Are my motives wrong? Am I asking You to be a genie? I have heard You in my anxiety and in my trouble. Will I hear you when my mind is not troubled? Would You speak to me today? What is my daily bread?* Then, like blessed rain during a severe drought, I heard Him speak. "Haste and delay do not exist for me. My timing is as perfect as My plan. My timing perfectly coincides with My path." I stopped and took in the words and thought, *Is that enough for me or do I want more? Lord, I will be satisfied with that, but I long for more. I long to hear more of Your voice* today *and every day. What else do I need to learn today? How am I not crying aloud to You as David does in Psalm 3? How am I running from you as Jonah does in Jonah 1? I know You hear me! I know You tell me to ask! Will you answer me today?* And God answered, "You put Me in a box when you face challenges. You view Me as contained and small. I am never hasty, and I never delay. Wait on Me. Trust Me. In those times, instead of putting Me in the box, put your circumstances in the 'waiting on the Lord' box." *With conviction I cry to You, "my circumstances do not change Your character." My challenges do not challenge Your capacity to handle them. As my enemies or trials grow, You remain constant in size and might. You are not careless but careful and deliberate. You do not cast me aside. My circumstances do not carry me away; You carry me through. You commune with me. I am cocooned in your comforting shield. I am cherished. Thank you, Lord!* Not only does God show me who He is and how He loves me, but He reveals *me* to me, the hidden things that I do not even know are buried in my heart. He shows me the lies and fears that I harbor, even when it appears to me that no lies or fears remain.

One of the biggest lies is that I do not fit in, that I am an outsider looking in, so I separate myself from groups. Out of obedience to God, I have been trying to navigate relationships and situations that I spent years avoiding. I have heard God clearly instructing me to stop being the separator, to cease being filled with disdain and anger towards people, to work on the bitterness that has taken root, and to stop being apathetic because it is easier for me to reject than to be rejected. While I am not anxious, I feel old and worn when it comes to community. I feel vulnerable and fragile. Instead of the joy of restoration with camaraderie and peace, I am exhausted. It feels like I am subjecting myself to the same old hurts, continually venturing into the painful places that caused me to close off from people in the first place. This is not a new struggle. This has been an attack for as long as I can remember. As I read Psalm 3, where David experienced his enemies pressing in, I am comforted. I love reading Psalms and engaging with the emotions that come with the hardness of life. I love knowing that we can continually hand these hard things over to God. Psalm 3 says, "O LORD, how many are my foes! Many are rising against me; many are saying of my soul, "There is no salvation for him in God." But you, O LORD, are a shield about me, my glory, and the lifter of my head. I cried aloud to the LORD, and he answered me from his holy hill. I lay down and slept; I woke again, for the LORD sustained me. I will not be afraid of the many thousands of people who have set themselves against me all around. Arise, O LORD! Save me, O my God! For you strike all my enemies on the cheek; you break the teeth of the wicked. Salvation belongs to the LORD; your blessing be on your people!"

While God's instruction is simple, battling my sinful heart and navigating relationships with others who have sinful hearts proves extremely challenging. It is a downward spiral of hurting and being hurt. I ignore or hurt others because they continue to hurt me. They hurt me because I continue to hurt them. Through the onslaught and the pain, I can become so caught up in what is going on around me that all I see is the difficulty and I hide from it. Psalms, such as this one, remind me of some truths about dealing with trials that renew our strength and encourage me to, once again, to put my trust in the Lord. I am reminded that I should cry aloud to the *Lord* for strength and guidance and not *everyone* else with my complaints. *Lord, You are my protection, and You remove my humiliation. I cry aloud to you today. Lord, if I am innocent, vindicate me. Lord, If I bear guilt, reveal it to me. Cleanse me!* I am reminded to trust in the Lord and not *everything* else. *No matter who or what is pressing in around me. No matter how bleak relationships look, things are going exactly according to your plan. Lord, I trust Your promise that You are working everything to the good of those who love You and are called according to Your purpose.* I am reminded that peace comes from the Lord and not *anything* else. Because God is always with us, peace is as readily found in the valley of the shadow of death as it is found in the green pastures. Our hearts and minds are guarded beyond human understanding by the Lord. *Lord, thank You for sustaining me and bringing peace to my heart so I can rest well.* Lastly, I know that safety and protection come from the Lord and *nothing* else. I do not need to fear one or thousands who are seeking to devour me, because if God is for me, who can be against me? I can pray, "God, break the teeth of the wicked. While they still may snarl and bite, render it ineffective to harm me." *God, I need You to remind me again that I am seen and loved. Remind me that I am set apart and that You have made me exactly as I am for a purpose and that I am your beautiful creation. Prevent me from crawling back into the darkness and hiding. Remind me that difficulty and suffering for Your sake is joyous and a privilege. I fail when I continue in my own strength. I need you to renew my strength, and I need to soar on your wings. I need to trust your ways and not lean on my own understanding. I can do all things through Christ who gives me strength, but I can do nothing without You. If I experience the same result from the same people a hundred more times, you will meet me in my need all one hundred times and provide exactly what I need to bring honor and glory to Your name.*

On day four, I was in Psalm 4 and Jonah 1. Feelings of anger and continued disappointment that I am not valued and respected by others were on my heart. My mouth runs rampant against people that I perceive disrespect me. The question on my heart was, *Lord, what do you want me to learn today?* Psalm 4:7 reminds me that "You have put more joy in my heart than they have when their grain and wine abound." This reality is a great reminder to show compassion and love. Satisfaction on my worst day surpasses satisfaction on their best day. *My joy is in You, God, not in the respect and reverence of my peers. My value and worth are in Christ. You are goodness supreme. You are my security. I am set apart in you. Let my soul be still. Do not let me sin in my anger. Do not let me speak lies. Let me ponder and be silent. Let me offer right sacrifices. Save me, Lord, from my own evil, selfish desires. Satisfy me, LORD, with your goodness.*

On day five, I was focused on Psalm 5 and Luke 14:25–35. Putting God first and intentionally listening well were on my heart, even though there was much to be done in my home because I was trying to finish eight costumes for my son's play. The question on my heart for God was, *What do you want me to learn today through Your Word?* Psalm 5:3 impacted me. Psalm 5:3 says, "O LORD, in the morning you hear my voice; in the morning I prepare a sacrifice for you and watch." It reminded me to set the correct tone of priority in the morning, every morning—to meet with God and speak with Him and then to prepare a sacrifice of my heart, to wait and watch expectantly for His voice and His will throughout my day. *Delight me, Lord, with your favor. Direct my steps. Let me dwell with You. Be my domicile. Daily, weed my life. Help me die to myself, so I can be Your disciple. Take my despair and my distress and my desires and help my eyes not be distorted. Prevent my enemies from destroying me, distracting me, deceiving me, distressing me, or devouring me. Help me be deliberate to seek You and depend on You.* I rest in the knowledge that the abundance of God's steadfast love is greater than the abundance of my enemies' transgressions. My responsibility is to sacrifice and wait expectantly, for God is a God who hears and moves. This verse was a reminder to me to take in God's Word every day and to ponder it throughout my day, no matter how busy my schedule and especially when others are demeaning towards me. It was a reminder to be diligent every day to surrender my life to Christ, cleaning and decluttering my heart, to imitate the character of God in my daily routines. As Luke 14:33 says, "So therefore, any one of you who does not renounce all that he has cannot be my disciple."

On Day 6, I was in Psalm 6, where David cries out to God to be rescued from his enemies. I also found myself in 2 Corinthians 12:10, where Paul says, "For the sake of Christ, then, I am content with weaknesses, insults, hardships, persecutions, and calamities. For when I am weak, then I am strong." I considered the question, *What happens to the heart that experiences the abundance Christ has to offer?* It is content and restful in all situations. It overflows to such a magnitude that it spills over. Joy and love compel us to reach out to others to share the blessedness that we have received. My prayer for my own heart for almost a decade has been that it would stop listening to, and following, my own voice because my God speaks and I long to listen to His voice over my own, that I would stop building my own kingdom and my version of abundance because my God satisfies all my needs, and that I would stop determining my own worth and value because my God created my purposes before I was ever born.

~

PAUSE TO PRAISE AND PONDER:

God tells Moses, "I AM WHO I AM." How does God reveal Himself as I AM through His Word and in our lives?
Read Exodus 3:1-14.

Theme: The I AM makes Himself known.

Praise: How would you define the name I AM WHO I AM?

Brainstorming:
How do you view God too loftily?

- How do you view Him as cold and uncaring?
- When have you asked Him "why?"

How do you view God too lowly?

- What do you fear?
- What are you hiding?

How does God define mankind?

- What Bible passages can you draw from?

Get Creative:
- Create two columns. Label one column THE I Am IS... and label the

other column SO I AM. Write aspects of God's identity and then consider how that impacts your identity in Him.

Daily Bread: In what ways can you bring God praise? How has God personally pursued You? How has God personally made Himself known to you?

- Draw a drinking glass. Select a verse related to what God has revealed to you today as you pondered, that speaks truth to the ways and promises of God.
- Draw a sandwich.
  - On the bottom bun, praise God by writing how you know God as I AM.
  - Select a way that your view of God is skewed and write it in the meat portion of the sandwich. Ask God to reveal truth to you.
  - On the top bun, write a truth contained in God's Word that combats your skewed perception of God and praise Him for it.

4

CALLED BY NAME

Exodus 3:4, "*When the* Lord *saw that he turned aside to see, God called him out of the bush, 'Moses, Moses!' and he said, 'Here I am.'*"

My husband's great-aunt Joyce oversaw the set and decorations of our church's Christmas concert every year for years. God called Joyce by name to paint and to artistically create beautiful things. She was special and known by God. She was a creative artist and visionary. I marveled at her talent and her ability to see things that did not yet exist. I marveled at her ministry of creating gorgeous God-centered environments. It was exciting to see things take shape, to see them come alive from her mind to her medium. One Sunday, our pastor was preaching on the artistry of God, on His love of beauty, on how God, Himself, is an artist of beautiful things as the creator of the world. As he spoke, Joyce was painting in the background. The entire service, we watched her paint a portrait of Jesus on the cross. I distinctly remember the painting because of its angle. As she painted the cross in comparison to Jesus's head and arms, the angle seemed drastically off, yet, as she completed it, I could see that it was perfect.

Towards the end of her life, she requested a candid picture of my children so she could paint them. Those were my busy mom years, the years full of too many things to do and a perpetual state of exhaustion, where nothing but necessity was completed, and the opportunity passed us by. With grief, I mourned her loss and the loss of a painting that only ever existed in her mind. Close to a year after Joyce had passed away, her family was clearing out her remaining paintings that no one in the immediate family had claimed. They were offering what was left to the extended family. Without my knowledge, my husband went over to select a few items. As he was going, he tried calling me to see what types of her paintings I would want but was not able to get ahold of me. If I had known he was calling me, I would have said, "ANY! Whatever you can get your hands on." After all, who am I to have a choice? I am the wife of a great nephew, an extended relation by marriage. I was so grateful to be offered anything. But, if I had been able to pick, I would have selected the painting that I watched her paint all those years ago. The one of Jesus on the cross, where the perspective looked completely off but, once finished, was perfect!

Has God ever delighted you in such a way that you know He knows the deepest parts of you? I am talking about one of those beautiful gifts from God that shows he knows your desires and delights to delight you, not by granting your every desire as if He is a servant who must obey your whims but as a Father that bestows gifts to His children simply to please them. God knows me. He knows my name. He knows my unnamed desires. My husband came home informing me that he had been trying to get ahold of me. He had several paintings and among them was the painting of Jesus on the cross with the cross behind Jesus's head at an upward angle. Every time I look at that painting hanging on my living room wall, I picture that sermon. I picture Joyce painting that painting and I see God's love of beauty and art displayed through the talent He blessed her with. God called Joyce by name, giving her a special calling to bring honor and glory to Himself.

The Bible reveals to us that the restoration of sight was a miracle that was reserved for God's Messiah. John 9:32 says, "Never since the world began has it been heard that anyone opened the eyes of a man born blind." Only God's Messiah, God incarnate, opens our eyes to receive sight, to understand that He calls us to Him through His sacrifice and grace. As Jesus declared in Luke 4:18, "The Spirit of the Lord is upon me, because he has anointed me to proclaim the good news to the poor. He has sent me to proclaim liberty to the captives and recovering of sight to the blind, to set at liberty those who are oppressed."

God calls us by name. It is only because He makes Himself known, by calling us to Him, that we can know Him. We cannot pridefully claim that we have goodness or wisdom within ourselves when this mystery has been revealed to our hearts. It is God who comes to us, calls us by restoring our sight, and makes Himself known to us. It is He who establishes our works and purposes, so we have nothing to boast about or grab ahold of in pride. As Paul asked in 1 Corinthians 4:7b, "What do you have that you did not receive? If then you received it, why do you boast as if you did not receive it?" It is all God working in us and through us to change us. Romans 11:36 says, "For from him and through him and for him are all things. To him be glory forever. Amen." What a blessed paradox that our efforts matter when it is entirely God moving and working in our hearts, but it is a blessing, indeed, to explore and discover.

Through His life-giving words, God restores knowledge and sight to the blind. Matthew 11:5 describes Jesus's ministry this way: "The blind receive their sight and the lame walk, lepers are cleansed and the deaf hear, and the dead are raised up, and the poor have good news preached to them." It is God who turns the dial of the microscope for us; He refocuses the lens and enhances our sight. For the first time, blurriness has dissipated, and we can recognize and see the truth through His Son. Yet, we still lack the crispness of sight that once was. We make out truth. We recognize Him and our need for Him, but because we are still sinful flesh, we have not yet learned to fully trust Him and follow His ways. We are like the man in the gospel of Mark whose sight has been restored yet is still blurry. Mark 8:23–25 describes his condition and full healing: "And he took the blind man by the hand and led him out of the village, and when he had spit on his eyes and laid his hands on him, he asked him, 'Do you see anything?' And he looked up and said, 'I see people, but they look like trees, walking.' Then Jesus laid his hand on his eyes again; and he opened his eyes, his sight was restored, and he saw everything clearly." As we are rescued by God, we receive sight, but our sight is still a little skewed. Our knowledge is not complete. As Jesus intervenes to fully restore the clarity of this man's sight, God acts to crisply and fully restore our sight. *God, restore my sight so that I may know you and may fully see the deceit contained in my heart. Help me to know you. Help me to know who you have called me to be.*

God is a relational God who calls and gives purpose to our lives. He hears. He sees both the oppression of the Egyptians and the affliction of the Israelites. He knows our names. He answers our cries for deliverance, and He sends help. He could act on His own, destroying the wicked and sparing the righteous, but instead, He not only reveals His plan of rescue to Moses but He also selects Moses to take part in His deliverance with Him. God deliberately draws near to and pursues Moses because Moses is special to God, known by Him. He captures the attention of the one who was drawn from the water and calls him by name, "Moses, Moses!"

This baby, who was beautiful in God's sight (Acts 7:20), was being prepared his entire life for this purpose. He was spared from the watery depths, brought into and protected in the home of Pharaoh, and instructed in all the wisdom of the Egyptians, all for a God-given purpose. All those years ago, he sensed that God was using him to deliver the people from slavery, and it was true. Somehow, Moses knew (Acts 7:24–26)! God calls him by name and sends him back to Egypt to deliver God's people by directing them through the water of the Red Sea. Exodus 14:21–22 describes this event this way, "Then Moses stretched out his hand over the sea, and the LORD drove the sea back by a strong east wind all night and made the sea dry land, and the waters were divided. And the people of Israel went into the midst of the sea on dry ground, the waters being a wall to them on their right hand and on their left."

Moses experiences God as God faithfully walks him through the miraculous. Moses records God's faithfulness despite his own doubt and fear. As he carries out what God has called him to, he realizes that God knows him completely, even the broken pieces. God walks him through every bit of doubt, fear, and faithlessness. God's mercies never fail Moses. They are new every morning. As the prophet Jeremiah said in Lamentations 3:22–23, "The steadfast love of the LORD never ceases; his mercies never come to an end; they are new every morning; great is your faithfulness." Then Moses shares his experiences with us, so that we can know this amazing, faithful, sending God as well. His words show us that there are so many wonderful things to learn about our God and King and that being led through the things that are hard and the things that seem impossible is worth it to know this amazing God.

God shows Moses and the Israelites that He will accomplish what He sets out to do. God's power is so great that He will be victorious despite Pharaoh's refusal to let His people go. He is so mighty that not only will they leave but the Israelites will also plunder the Egyptians on their way out. He reveals His control over life and death and His superiority over the Egyptian gods through the ten plagues, and yet, through His powerful might and judgment, God's mercy beautifully shines forth. He provides a way for lives to be spared from the angel of death through a sacrificial lamb.

God does not stop with Moses. We see God call Aaron, whom later Jews would call the "light bringer", by name and send him into the wilderness.[1] Aaron was also special and known by God. It was God who asked, when Moses was afraid of speaking before Pharaoh, "Is there not Aaron, your brother, the Levite? I know that he can speak well" (Exodus 4:14). Unlike Moses, we see no hesitation by Aaron to fulfill what God called him to do. Exodus 4:27 tells us, "The LORD said to Aaron, 'Go into the wilderness and meet Moses.' So he went and met him at the mountain of God and kissed him." Through Aaron, God reveals to the people of Israel that He will deliver them from slavery, that He will redeem them with an outstretched arm and with great acts of judgment (Exodus 4:30–31, 6:6). God then shares that He will fulfill the promise given to Abraham, and that He will bring this people into their own land. Aaron faithfully says and performs all the signs that Moses told him, and the people believe and worship God (Exodus 4:30–31).

All too quickly, the belief and worship of the people is snuffed out. The severity of the harsh labor put upon them stresses these people to the breaking point. Exodus 6:9 says, "Moses spoke thus to the people of Israel, but they did not listen to Moses, because of their broken spirit and harsh slavery." Instead of labeling their hearts as weak and fickle, imagine being subjected to an all-consuming oppression in such a way. Imagine being so browbeaten that there is no longer any capacity to even consider hope. That strikes as poignant in my heart as I look around at the hopelessness in

---

1. "H175—Aharon—Strong's Hebrew Lexicon (KJV)," BlueLetterBible, https://www.blueletterbible.org/lexicon/h175/kjv/wlc/0-1/.

our society, as people unknowingly grasp at their oppressive chains for deliverance, removing their capacity to consider the hope that God offers. We observe through these people just how feebly we hold onto Him. Yet, it allows us to comprehend just how completely and firmly God upholds us. The actions of God are amazing—full of mercy, grace, and steadfast love. Regardless of the Israelites' belief and worship or their deafness and distraction, God continues to move His plan of rescue forward. He solidly upholds us because we are wobbly. God does not require an instantaneous, all-in, unshakable faith. His grace allows us the room to expand our faith, to come to know Him more deeply after He reveals Himself to us. He does not expect us to automatically know how to live by faith and not by sight. He tests and stretches our faith and teaches us how to trust Him more completely.

The people of Israel were special and known by God. They were set apart by Him when God called Abram and promised him a nation. God calls the people of Israel ("God prevails") by name. Genesis 32:28 is the first use of this name: "And he said, 'Your name shall no longer be called Jacob, but Israel, for you have striven with God and with men, and have prevailed.'" When Jacob's name was changed, he asks the Lord to reveal his name. Genesis 32:29 says, "Then Jacob asked him, 'Please tell me your name.' But he said, 'Why is it that you ask my name?' And there he blessed him." Similarly, when Moses is called, he asks the Lord His name. We see that when God calls us, He is not only revealing He knows us, but He is making Himself known to us. As He makes Himself known to us, He begins moving in our lives. God is calling these people from a land of slavery to become His special, set-apart people, to live in obedience to Him in the land of promise. Exodus 12:41 indicates this with a special description of the people of Israel as the "hosts of the LORD", "At the end of 430 years, on that very day, all the hosts of the LORD went out from the land of Egypt." God's favor was upon them. The world would see the blessing of God upon these people and, as Egypt discovered, nations that went up against them would be cursed by God. Isaiah 43:1–2 uses vivid imagery to describe this favor and blessing: "But now thus says the LORD, he who created you, O Jacob, he who formed you, O Israel: 'Fear not, for I have redeemed you; I have called you by name, you are mine. When you pass through the waters, I will be with you; and through the rivers, they shall not overwhelm you; when you walk through fire you shall not be burned, and the flame shall not consume you.'" But it is in the next verses that we understand why. Isaiah 43:3a continues, "For I am the LORD your God, the Holy One of Israel, your Savior." And Isaiah 43:4a adds, "Because you are precious in my eyes, and honored, and I love you." God does more than just tell us about Himself; He allows us to experience Him. The arm of the Lord reaches down and upholds us, rescuing us from the pit. Being called by name goes beyond rescue from darkness; it involves stepping into the light, not because of our own grandness but so we can know God and His grandness.

Some calls are not directly spoken, sending directives by God. Sometimes our calling is in the ordinary course of our day. We may not even realize we are being called to something. We are simply living out our lives, but we are called and known nonetheless. In Jeremiah 1:5, God says this is true of Jeremiah: "Before I formed you in the womb I knew you, and before you were born, I consecrated you; I appointed you a prophet to the nations." Some calls are to stand firm with what God has already entrusted us with. By name, God called the midwives, Shiphrah and Puah, to stand firm in faith. These two women, whose names mean "fair" and "splendid", were special and known by God.[2] They lived in a manner worthy of their names. They were seen, protected, and favored by God. Exodus 1:15–17 describes their actions: "Then the king of Egypt said to the Hebrew midwives, one of whom was named Shiphrah and the other Puah, 'When you serve as midwife to the Hebrew women and see them on the birthstool, if it is a son, you shall kill him, but if it is a daughter, she shall live.' But the midwives feared God and did not do as the king of Egypt commanded them, but let the male children live." These women born to help bring life into the world were being asked to destroy life. Instead of fear driving them to behave outside of the purpose that God gave them, they courageously held firm to what they knew to be true, and God rewarded them for it. Exodus 1:20 tells us, "So God dealt well with the midwives. And the people multiplied and grew very strong." These power-

2. H8236—Šiprâ—Strong's Hebrew Lexicon (KJV)," BlueLetterBible, https://www.blueletterbible.org/lexicon/h175/kjv/wlc/0-1/; H6326—Pû 'âh— Strong's Hebrew Lexicon (KJV)," BlueLetterBible, https://www.blueletterbible.org/lexicon/h6326/kjv/wlc/0-1/

less servants in Egypt were fearless in facing what Pharaoh, the most powerful person in the land, would do to them, whereas the Pharaoh, who wielded all the power, was riddled with fear. We see God call them by name to stand firm in the middle of life's difficult circumstances. Have you ever wondered what the ripple effect of these two women standing firm may have had on the rest of Israel's story? How did these women affect the congregation of Israel? What men lived and how did they impact the congregation? Their choices mattered beyond their acts of faith and steadfastness due to every life who lived because of their courage. In what ways did their faith and defiance of the king's orders encourage others to dare to defy the orders of Pharaoh also?

Each of these examples is God working out His plan, allowing people the privilege of making ripples of influence in one another's stories. Sometimes these ripples make an impression of influence, and sometimes these ripples rescue us. Take the life of Moses: his deliverance story rippled from the choices of three different women. God used the faithfulness of Jochebed in defying the law of the land, and, as a result, Moses's life was spared. She saw the beauty of this child and chose life despite the consequences. He used the compassion of Pharaoh's daughter to rescue him, when Moses could not rescue himself and when he could not be rescued by his own family. And He used the courage of a young girl who willingly drew near enough to see what would happen to her brother and to speak up when the right moment came. Like how God has created the church to move and act in unity, the result of the action of all three of them, unknowingly working in unity, was rescue.

Moses shows us by example that revelation from God is different from knowing God. God introduces himself to Moses, but it will take time for Moses to know God. Like a courtship, where the beginning of a relationship consists of sharing about ourselves, only time spent together allows us to truly know one another. Moses begins his journey with hesitation. He starts by being focused on himself and by questioning God but ends his days as a completely changed individual, as a man who relinquishes all other things and rests on the promises of God. To shift from the revelation of God to properly knowing God, it is important to observe what God has revealed about Himself without presuppositions, to absorb not only what we observe from the Scriptures, but to apply that to what we experience in life, to allow it to take root in our hearts to become knowledge. How often do we claim God as our own while we also contort Him to fit into the mold that we have created for him to best suit our purposes? Instead of seeking to know Him for who He is, we fit Him around who we would like Him to be.

As God met Moses on the mountaintop of Sinai after the exodus from Egypt, the first thing that God said about Himself is that He is merciful and gracious. Exodus 34:6-7 tells us, "The LORD passed before him and proclaimed, 'The LORD, the LORD, a God merciful and gracious, slow to anger, and abounding in steadfast love and faithfulness, keeping steadfast love for thousands, forgiving iniquity and transgression and sin, but who will by no means clear the guilty, visiting the iniquity of the fathers on the children and the children's children, to the third and fourth generation.'" But this promise of God is not only told to His people Israel; it is shown to every child of God over and over—daily, weekly, monthly, and over the course of our lives. His mercy reigns over our faith. When we stumble and fall, God lovingly carries us through. Mercy does what is best for you even when you do not have the strength to do it for yourself.

God allows the Israelites to hear His words from Moses and Aaron, "I AM has sent me to you . . . The LORD, the God of your fathers, the God of Abraham, the God of Isaac, and the God of Jacob, has sent me to you . . . I have observed you and what has been done to you in Egypt, and I promise that I will bring you up out of the affliction of Egypt to the land of the Canaanites, the Hittites, the Amorites, the Perizzites, the Hivites, and the Jebusites, a land flowing with milk and honey" (Exodus 3:14–16) Then God shows them that His words hold true, that His words are trustworthy. God stretches out His hand and strikes Egypt with nine plagues, and He allows Israel to witness His might, but there comes a time where we are all called to stop being onlookers and bystanders to God's miracles and we are called to become people who walk by faith. We see this change with the tenth plague, the death of the firstborn, and God's accompanying protective ceremony, Passover. All the congregation of Israel was to take the blood of the lambs that they had brought into their households and put it on the doorposts and lintels of their houses. God gives this warning and direction in Exodus 12:12–13, "For I will pass through the land of Egypt that night, and I will strike all the firstborn in the land of Egypt, both man and beast;

and on all the gods of Egypt I will execute judgments: I am the LORD. The blood shall be a sign for you, on the houses where you are. And when I see the blood, I will pass over you, and no plague will befall you to destroy you, when I strike the land of Egypt."

God delivers, God spares, God feeds, God leads, and God dwells among these people. Instead of overwhelming gratitude and unshakable loyalty, we see discontented faithlessness. The psalmist Asaph writes in Psalm 78:15–20, using the wilderness years as a warning to his own time, "He split rocks in the wilderness and gave them drink abundantly as from the deep. He made streams come out of the rock and caused waters to flow down like rivers. Yet they sinned still more against him, rebelling against the Most High in the desert. They tested God in their heart by demanding the food that they craved. They spoke against God, saying, 'Can God spread a table in the wilderness? He struck the rock so that water gushed out and streams overflowed. Can he also give bread or provide meat for his people?'" Yet, even with the complaining and malcontentedness, the desire of the people to return to Egypt, the accusations against God and Moses that they had been brought out to the desert to die, and the crafting of a golden calf to worship (in which they shockingly claimed, "This is your God who brought you up out of Egypt"), God does not abandon them. He still claims them as His people. He chooses to remain with them and to dwell among them, even as the generation of the Israelites who left Egypt remained in the desert and did not enter the Promised Land in their disobedience. God's commitment is evident in Exodus 33:14, "And he said, 'My presence will go with you, and I will give you rest.'"

Those God calls by name He does not forsake. His graciousness and mercy ensure that He remains despite our sinfulness. Nehemiah 9 captures the fickle history of the Israelites and God's absolute graciousness and mercy towards them. It reveals God's mercy cycle towards His people, a pattern of God graciously giving, their abuse of the gift, their turning away, the consequence for the behavior, their repentance and crying out for rescue, and then merciful rescue and deliverance once more. What moves a God, who is abounding in mercy, to swallow up His enemies? How utterly unyielding must people be for a God longing to extend mercy to hand them over to destruction?

In Nehemiah 9:33, the leaders of the Levites recognize the truth: "Yet you have been righteous in all that has come upon us, for you have dealt faithfully and we have acted wickedly." God's mercy does not run dry when He denies this people entrance into the Promised Land. His mercy does not evaporate when He later scatters the established nation due to their disobedience. God's warnings and His consequences are a demonstration of His love and His mercy. God delivers one such warning about a day of judgment in Ezekiel 7:9, "And my eye will not spare, nor will I have pity. I will punish you according to your ways, while your abominations are in your midst. Then you will know that I am the LORD, who strikes." Lovingly, albeit sternly, God is ever reminding and showing each generation that He alone is God, and sometimes reminding requires striking with consequences. God's love in the face of rebellion is illustrated in Nehemiah 9:16–21, "But they and our fathers acted presumptuously and stiffened their neck and did not obey your commandments. They refused to obey and were not mindful of the wonders that you performed among them, but they stiffened their neck and appointed a leader to return to their slavery to Egypt. But you are a God ready to forgive, gracious and merciful, slow to anger and abounding in steadfast love, and did not forsake them. Even when they had made for themselves a golden calf and said, 'This is your God who brought you up out of Egypt,' and had committed great blasphemies, you in your great mercies did not forsake them in the wilderness. The pillar of cloud to lead them in the way did not depart from them by day, nor the pillar of fire by night to light for them the way by which they should go. You gave your good Spirit to instruct them and did not withhold your manna from their mouth and gave them water for their thirst. Forty years you sustained them in the wilderness, and they lacked nothing. Their clothes did not wear out and their feet did not swell."

God's mercies and His presence remain with the next generation as they are about to enter the land. In Deuteronomy 4:31, Moses reminds them, "For the Lord your God is a merciful God. He will not leave you or destroy you or forget the covenant with your fathers that he swore to them." God bestows upon them every corner of the promised inheritance (Nehemiah 9:22). His mercy remains with the people of Israel who inhabited the land. In Nehemiah 9:24–25, the Levites recall, "So the descendants went in and possessed the land, and you subdued before them the inhabitants of the land, the Canaanites, and gave them into their hand, with their kings and the peoples of the land, that they might do with them as they would. And they captured fortified cities and a rich land, and took possession of houses full of all good things, cisterns already hewn, vineyards, olive orchards and fruit trees in abundance. So they ate and were filled and became fat and delighted themselves in your great goodness."

Due to their disobedience and the killing of God's prophets, however, they were later scattered by their enemies, and still God mercifully warns them and guides them. 2 Chronicles 30:9 records this motivation for repentance in a letter from Hezekiah, "For if you return to the LORD, your brothers and your children will find compassion with their captors and return to this land. For the LORD your God is gracious and merciful and will not turn away his face from you, if you return to him." Despite all their wickedness and their turning away from Him, God never destroys His people nor forsakes them because of His gracious and merciful nature (Nehemiah 9:31). There is always a remnant spared. He is angry because of their infidelity, but His heart longs to restore and forgive. One of God's final prophecies before 400 years of silence is Malachi 3:17, "They shall be mine, says the LORD of hosts, in the day when I make up my treasured possession, and I will spare them as a man spares his son who serves him." He knows us as we really are—all our frailty and fickleness—and He chooses us despite it. God sees us as a new creation, fully restored, how we were always meant to be, as our truest version of ourselves. Paul recognizes this in 2 Corinthians 5:17, where he says, "Therefore, if anyone is in Christ, he is a new creation. The old has passed away; behold, the new has come."

I had a dream that I worked with my husband. In this dream my coworkers were bad-mouthing him to our boss and it was affecting his reputation with her, so I approached her defending him against their verbal attack. She was allowing me to speak, but I could tell that she was not really listening to what I had to say. I knew that her opinion of him had already been skewed, that she believed my coworkers over me. As can only occur in dreams, as I was speaking with her, I became aware of the fact that I needed to go with the pastor of my church to speak with a woman about an extremely important and sensitive matter. As I was talking to my manager, my pastor approached me so we could meet her together, and I found myself very torn. I really wanted to go with him to handle this situation and to help this woman, but I was also not ready to finish my conversation with my manager until my own personal matter was resolved. I was so preoccupied with defending my husband that I was not properly focusing on this woman's situation or prayerfully considering what we were going to say to her, like I should have been. I was so consumed with defending him that it was not until we approached her that the depths of my negligence towards her registered. As we approached her, I realized I was not sure that I even knew her name. Panicked, I was trying to remember, and I was questioning whether I had it right. As we reached her, I quietly called her Emily and then second-guessed myself and more loudly called her Kate. At that point, my pastor corrected me with disappointment and said, "Her name is Emily."

As I woke up, I realized that this dream represented anxiety and fears I was harboring in my heart regarding the publishing of my book and that God gave me a beautiful reassurance through this dream. First, the coworkers and my boss in this dream were actual people in my life who I have worked with. They represent to me people who tend to focus on appearances over the heart. I always struggled in that work environment, because this manager always seemed to appreciate the "show" over my authentic heart offering. My pleasing, perfectionist heart wanted the same measure of validation and favor. During my years of service, I had to constantly remind myself to focus on God for my value and worth and not on my manager's approval. The attack on my husband in this dream spoke of my deep-rooted fear of how my family would be assessed from the release of the book. What would the attack and ramifications be? My pastor is a man of God whom I respect and have learned a great deal from. He has not read my book, and, if I am honest, I become anxious when I imagine him doing so. This points to needing his affirmation, which I admit is both good and bad. It is good to long to receive affirmation from someone who follows God, who is so knowledgeable about His Word, and who can validate that my book is grounded in truth. It is bad to focus all my energy and attention on what someone else thinks of me, on trying to earn their favor, that I am so desperate for affirmation that when I reveal all the ugliness and brokenness inside me in a desire to bring honor and glory to God, I wince when I imagine a loving man of God reading it.

The one aspect of my dream which did not make sense was the names of the woman we were meeting. She was not someone I knew outside of my dream. All I knew about her in the dream was that she had a problem that I needed to speak with her about. When I woke up, I thought, "Why the names *Emily* and *Kate*?" I do not know any Emilys or any Kates. So, I looked up the meaning of these names. *Emily* means *rival* or *laborious* and *Kate* means *pure*. It struck me. Wow! Those names capture the essence of God's transformation in my life. Laboring has always been my way—to please, appear well, perform, be perfect—so much so that it was even evidenced by my actions in this dream. I was rivaling so constantly with my flashy, showy coworkers, wanting to stand out, that it affected my ability to focus on, and reach out to, those who are in need. My envy completely overshadowed my ability to care for others and mirrors the natural bent of my heart and, sadly, the truth of the course of my life on many occasions. I am too consumed with my own problems and discomfort to see the needs of anyone else, always wanting to be acknowledged for being the best and seeking to be the best.

I am currently in the transformation process of going from Emily, someone defined by her "laborious and rivaling" ways, to Kate, one who rests in being "pure." And by sharing my struggles and my story, I pray that I encourage others to leave pit-dwelling Emily behind and venture forth into the light, embracing their God-given pure identity of Kate. During this process I was trying to be bold and obedient. I was trying to keep my fears and anxiety at bay and, in courage, trust God. I was trying to be still, to act in the knowledge that He is God. I thought I was succeeding, and in my sleep, the truth of the depths of my anxiety within my spirit surfaced. I praise God for this dream, so I could once again hand my fears over to Him.

While this dream spoke to me and I was spiritually able to connect to both the names *Emily* and *Kate*, neither of those names are my name. My name is Angela René, a name that is rarely remembered. My entire life I have been called April or Andrea, and while those are lovely names, neither of them are *my* name. I have heard countless times, "I'm sorry, what was your name again?" There is something so devaluing about being nameless and faceless to everyone around you. To call someone by the wrong name, in my dream, is a deeply wounding thing to do to someone. It goes beyond simply not remembering. It reflects not seeing that person. It signifies that that person is of little significance to my life. That sentiment was affirmed by my actions in my dream, as my focus centered on defending my husband, whose reputation reflects on mine, over the heart and well-being of this woman I was entrusted with caring for. How often is this our reality and not a dream? We cannot fully commit to seeing and meeting the needs of others because we are too focused on how we appear to someone else that we deem more worthy of our time and energy. *Lord, teach me to lay aside my Emily tendencies and fully step into being Kate, a pure follower, who can step into your good purposes for my life.*

Sometimes I sit in the quiet of the morning, reading my Bible and drinking coffee with my mug that reads, "I have called you by name." My name is Angela, meaning *angelic.* I always wince a little bit when I tell people the meaning of my name. Ironically, it represents what I have always striven to achieve but have never been able to measure up to. If people saw what was lurking deep down inside of me, they would see anything but the perfect little angel I have always striven to be.

During the year I was prayerfully considering what I needed to be ready for, I found myself, yet again, rivaling, struggling, and comparing my offering of service against another person's. In this season of waiting, as God was teaching me what boldness in humility and love looks like, my bold steps left a past wound open and exposed, and this exposed wound was reinjured through the unintentional and unknowing actions of others, as I felt overlooked while a sister in Christ was embraced. Jealousy deep in my core was exposed, revealing yet another way that I am not a perfect angel. A dear friend was encouraging me and talking to me in my struggle, and she gave me life-giving words in a simple and true statement. She reminded me that my name means "messenger of God". Whoa! What a blessed and beautiful reminder that God has called me by name and given me a purpose that has nothing to do with my perfection and everything to do with His perfection.

Our purposes can so easily be skewed by the influence of the world. It turns the messenger of the Holy One, the only One worthy of worship, into the holy thing to be worshipped. It is the world that has given angels their current connotation by means of lies and misrepresentation, dark lies masked as light and hope. The world has turned these messengers of God into the angelic, perfect, innocent winged celestial beings strumming harps, and it has resulted in skewing their true purpose and identity which is to carry out the message of God. Somewhere my identity took on the same skewed image of light and perfection, while my purpose all along has been to share the good news of the gospel of Jesus Christ.

My middle name, René, means *reborn*, which is exactly the identity that Jesus's gift of grace has given me. From before I was born, God has claimed me to be His reborn messenger. This is a solid, valid claim that my value and worth in His eyes cannot be taken away from me. He called me by name. I am special and known by God, intended to complete His special purpose for me. I willingly relinquish the perfect, angelic identity that I tried to assume and that drove me to labor, without purpose, in vain. I marvel that God chooses the unseen girl, the girl without a voice, to be His messenger. Until I was reborn, my message was distorted and silent. Now that God has brought me new life, I am learning to be a true, authentic, and bold messenger of God.

~

PAUSE TO PRAISE AND PONDER:

Theme: To recognize that God has called us by name for His righteous purposes.
Read Exodus 3:1–14.

Brainstorming:
How would others describe you?
How would you describe yourself?
What do you feel you were born to do?
What hobbies or topics are life giving to you?

Get Creative:
- Write your full name on a name tag and then write what your full name means on another name tag.
-OR-

- Create a name tent. Write your full name on one side and the meaning of your full name on the other side.
- Using each letter in the name EMILY, what rivalrous and striving behaviors is God calling your attention to?
- Using the letters in the name KATE, how is God asking you to abide?

Mirror:
How do you personally connect with the meaning of your name?
How do you not connect with the meaning of your name?
How is God calling you by name today? What is He asking you to step toward?
Remember, Moses knew his identity long before God called him by name. How is God asking you to wait on His timing to fulfill what He has in store for you?

Daily Bread: In what ways can you bring God praise? How is God personally calling you? What word, phrase, action, or topic is He revealing to you?

- Draw a drinking glass. Select a verse related to what God has revealed to you today as you pondered that speaks the truth about the ways and promises of God.
- Draw a sandwich.
    - On the bottom bun, praise God by writing how you know that God is a personal God who calls us by name.
    - Select one way that you know God has called you by name or select one way that you are trying to discern that God is calling you by name and write it in the meat section of the sandwich. Ask God for wisdom and discernment in how to move.
    - On the top bun, write a truth contained in God's Word that explains how you may be being called by name.

5

LAYING DOWN THE SERPENT

Exodus 4:2–4, "*The* Lord *said to him, 'What is that in your hand?' He said, 'A staff.' And he said, 'Throw it on the ground.' So he threw it on the ground, and it became a serpent, and Moses ran from it. But the* Lord *said to Moses, 'Put out your hand and catch it by the tail'—so he put out his hand and caught it, and it became a staff in his hand.*"

When I was young, I would occasionally ride roller coasters, but I was petrified of them. I would clamp my eyes closed and grasp tightly onto the bar and pray for the ride to be over as quickly as possible. It was miserable, but I would keep going on them to not appear weak or fearful in front of my siblings. One day, I decided to let go! I raised my hands and down the hill we flew. In that moment of letting go, I discovered my love of coasters. Somehow, as I physically let go of the bar, it loosened and let me let go of the fear inside. I learned to trust the restraints holding me and enjoy the ride. God, our Protector, is the restraint holding us that we come to understand if we loosen our grip and let go of the fear inside to follow the course that He has laid out for our lives.

Exodus 2:11–17 tells us, "One day, when Moses had grown up, he went out to his people and looked on their burdens, and he saw an Egyptian beating a Hebrew, one of his people. He looked this way and that, and seeing no one, he struck down the Egyptian and hid him in the sand. When he went out the next day, behold, two Hebrews were struggling together. And he said to the man in the wrong, 'Why do you strike your companion?' He answered, 'Who made you a prince and judge over us? Do you mean to kill me as you killed the Egyptian?' Then Moses was afraid, and thought, 'Surely the thing is known.' When Pharaoh heard of it, he sought to kill Moses. But Moses fled from Pharaoh and stayed in the land of Midian. And he sat down by a well. Now the priest of Midian had seven daughters, and they came and drew the water and filled the troughs to water their father's flock. The shepherds came and drove them away, but Moses stood up and saved them, and watered their flock."

We expect big things from this baby condemned to die who, instead of being cast down into the abyss, was drawn from the water, from this Hebrew slave who became a prince. After all, "Moses was instructed in all the wisdom of the Egyptians, and he was mighty in his words and deeds" (Acts 7:22). Yet, at the close of Exodus chapter 2, content to finally have a place to call home among the Midianites (Exodus 2:21), Moses's life is far from extraordinary. We find him living an imitation life, tending sheep. He has seemingly forgotten how salvation was to come by his hand. Instead of rescuing, he runs and hides. He forgets God's people in the aftermath of his failure. We expect noble, courageous acts and, instead, learn of murder, a cover-up, and a flight across the desert in fear.

Even at his lowest point, with no plan and no home, left with absolutely nothing, his very nature quickly resurfaces, and he delivers Jethro's daughters. Even though he has lost sight of it, we can clearly see that rescuing is what Moses was born to do. Moses steps in without hesitation because being a deliverer is in the fabric of his DNA. Yet over the course of time, he seems to forget this. This prince who looked upon his people looks away and settles into a life of mundane contentment. Meanwhile the people of Israel slave away without a deliverer to rescue them. At this moment, however, we see one of the most comforting and hopeful of all scriptures in the Bible. Exodus 2:25 says, "God saw the people of Israel—and God knew." No matter the heart and evil intent of someone like Pharaoh, no matter the disengaged heart of someone like Moses, God knows our plight and moves in response to it. At this moment, at this well (Exodus 2:15), as we gaze upon the paradox of this man, who looked like and had the wisdom of an Egyptian (Exodus 2:19), yet had the heart of a Hebrew, we see the life of Moses veering off his expected course into a new life. But God knows! God moves and I AM brings to be.

Mercifully, the loving, redemptive plan of God always moves His people toward deliverance. Graciously, the transformative plan of God refuses to let Moses continue to hide in his complacency, shame, failure, and fear. The God of Abraham, Isaac, and Jacob, who knows, approaches Moses and reminds him of His people's sufferings (Exodus 3:7). He calls Moses by name to bring the people out of the land. God calls him to step forward and accomplish what he was born to do. In Exodus 3:10, God says, "'Come, I will send you to Pharaoh that you may bring my people, the children of Israel, out of Egypt.'" God reveals Himself to Moses as I AM. But Moses has changed. Moses, who once had a heart for these people, who looked towards them, who knew that the salvation of his brothers was coming by his hand, does not jump at the chance to act.

Exodus 3:11–14 describes his response: "'But Moses said to God, "Who am I that I should go to Pharaoh and bring the children of Israel out of Egypt?' He said, 'But I will be with you, and this shall be the sign for you, that I have sent you: when you have brought the people out of Egypt, you shall serve God on this mountain.' Then Moses said to God, 'If I come to the people of Israel and say to them, 'The God of your fathers has sent me to you,' and they ask me, 'What is his name?' what shall I say to them?' God said to Moses, 'I AM WHO I AM.' And he said, 'Say this to the people of Israel: 'I AM has sent me to you.'" Instead of prompt obedience, Moses begins laying out his shortcomings to God. He no longer sees himself as a rescuer or deliverer. Moses has discovered and become intimately familiar with the failure within himself. He sees a sojourner, a killer, and a nobody, an unimpactful man who has neither the clout nor ability to say anything important to inspire anyone to listen to or heed him. Can you relate to Moses at this moment? I imagine my response to such a request if I were Moses: *"God, I already tried this, and nobody listened. My speech is slow, and I do not know what to say. I do not speak eloquently. People do not follow me. Who am I to be your voice? I am a failure who fled, not a rescuer and certainly not a leader. What I had to say before, when I was a prince, was ignored by the Hebrews. Why would they listen to me now when I am a nobody? What I did forced me to give up everything that I knew. My life is good now. I have finally found contentment. I belong. I do not want to give that up too. Please do not make me go back."* God, in His amazing patience and goodness, addresses Moses's shortcomings with His presence, and Moses's fears with God's own worthiness. We learn that it does not matter who you are. It matters Who is with you (Exodus 3:11–12). We also learn that it does not matter that you do not know what to say because God's name, I AM, is enough (Exodus 3:13–14).

I would imagine that fear for his safety would have topped Moses's list of why he does not want to go, but we do not see any indication of that in the text. He does not focus on his life. He focuses on not being heard. When we look at the concerns he lays out before God, Moses is more concerned with what to say, his inability to say it well, and whether he will be believed. Amazingly, nothing is said about his personal safety. Have you ever felt that there is something special within you and nobody cares or listens, so you venture out to make your mark? You are determined to do what you know you were born to do, and it fails; what then? What do you do when you find yourself at the death of a dream? Do we walk away and stop trying? Do we settle into what is comfortable? It is in the third concern he raises where we understand that Moses's hesitancy to move forward is due to the failures of his past. Exodus 4:1 gives his reply, "'But behold, they will not believe me or listen to my voice, for they will say, 'The LORD did not appear to you.'" As he utters these words to God, I imagine the words of the Hebrew slave from all those years ago echoing in his brain, "Who made you a prince and a judge over us? Do you mean to kill me as you killed the Egyptian?" (Exodus 2:14) I wonder how many times in the last forty years those words echoed in his brain, shaming and invalidating him, labeling him a murderer, not a rescuer. It must have been deeply significant, a moment that shaped Moses's view of himself, because it is the only recorded conversation that Moses took part in from his past, the only recorded words that were spoken directly to him from his early life.

Exodus 4:2-4 gives us God's answer, "The LORD said to him, 'What is that in your hand?' He said, 'A staff.' And he said, 'Throw it on the ground.' So, he threw it on the ground, and it became a serpent, and Moses ran from it. But the LORD said to Moses, 'Put out your hand and catch it by the tail'—so he put out his hand and caught it, and it became a staff in his hand." Once again, we find a kaleidoscope of amazing details in God's

Word that reveals absolute treasure. If we take the time to consider the significance of these details, we learn something truly amazing about our God and what He can do in our lives when He is with us and when He is sending us. God's response to him is not simply a show of might; it is a profound statement that should make us all take notice regarding our possessions, talents, abilities, even our failures and our weaknesses. Our glimpse into what has shaped the life and heart of Moses culminates in this moment where God directs Moses to lay down his staff.

The staff in Moses's hand, which God told him to lay down, was significant because not only was it a useful tool for Moses as he tended the sheep in the wilderness but it was also the only possession within Moses's grasp. It was literally the only thing that he was holding in his hand at that moment, not only representing Moses's newfound identity but also signifying all that Moses has to offer, and God tells him to lay it down. So, as Moses literally lays down this staff, he is figuratively laying down his purpose and identity, all that he is and all that he has, before God.

But, as it is laid down, it changes form. It is no longer a staff at all but a serpent. Of all the things for it to become as God is calling Moses into action with a sign, why would He choose a serpent? Anyone familiar with Genesis understands the slithering sliminess that comes with the serpent. Hearing of the appearance of a serpent in this beautiful, intimate moment between God and Moses makes us recoil, wondering why God has taken us back to that scene of ugliness, where separation from Him begins. Genesis 3:1 says, "Now the serpent was more crafty than any other beast of the field that the LORD God had made. He said to the woman, 'Did God actually say, 'You shall not eat of any tree in the garden?''" If I consider the vast array of things that God could have turned this staff into, why would He select the beast of the field which first introduced us to failures and fears? The reminder of the serpent seems like the least likely choice for God to use to encourage someone fearful to act. Instead of a gleaming light of reassurance to bolster our confidence, it seems to represent an obnoxious beacon of our failure, a reminder of how easily we believe the serpent's lies, distortion, deceit, and manipulation that led to our separation from God.

As Eve discovered, the serpent's lies are of the crafty, subtle variety, little lies that hold partial truths, slight, skewing lies that we are willing to nibble on and ingest, lies that become how we view ourselves and our identity, and lies that drive us to hide and wander aimlessly in the desert, just as Moses did, assuming a new, safer yet unsatisfying, unfulfilling identity. We choose contentment over abounding victory in God. Now an understanding of why the serpent needs to make an appearance in this moment comes into focus. The built-up, slithery, and crafty lies that Moses has consumed over the course of his life about who he really is need to be laid down—relinquished for Moses to move forward in faith. It is often not until we lay down whatever we are claiming and clutching tightly to that we recognize that the identity that we are clutching tightly to *is* the lie, that it is the instrument of death ready to strike its lethal blow, not the status symbol representing security and worth that we thought it was.

One way to render someone ineffective for the kingdom of God is to create doubt or, even better, fear of the identity that God has given that person to use for His purposes. It makes perfect sense that the serpent would attack identity. Attacking identity strikes at the very core of who we are. It is personal and hurtful. From the very beginning this has been the serpent's tactic. Consider the serpent's targeted attack on Adam and Eve's identities: their identities were captured in their names, meaning "man" and "life", and they were convinced by the serpent that they could be "god," while the consequence brought forth "death". As they grasp at the serpent's promise of identity, which was portrayed so amazingly, they find themselves opposite of God's purpose for them, losing their identities. Yet it is through their identities, "man" and "life," that the Messiah, our Savior, comes.

Moses's calling was not to shepherd mere sheep; his calling was to shepherd God's people. Imagine with me the burden that would have been released from Moses if he would have recognized that God was not only rescuing the Israelites from bondage but He was rescuing Moses as well. God was freeing him from the lies of his past, the lies that shrouded his worth and identity. Acts 7:23–25 teaches us that somehow Moses knew that God was going to use him to give the Israelites salvation. All those years ago, he moved, knowing his identity, to rescue these people, and when he tried, it did not happen. He failed. So, with failure comes self-effacement and doubt. We begin believing the lies that Satan hurls at us. We question whether we heard God correctly. Or worse, we question our worth. *Who am I to think that God would use me in this way? I am slow of speech and tongue* (Exodus 4:10). *How can I be of any use to God?* What does God say to past failures? "Lay down the deception, the doubt, and the lies that surround you. I am enough for you." But like Moses, we hold onto our self-made belief system established by our life experiences. We struggle to trust the One who has established our works. We hesitate to step toward what God has in store for us, what God has created us to be.

Sometimes the simplest way to fully understand a point is to look at its opposite. Let us look at someone who handled adversity differently. Immediately, my mind focuses on the life and actions of Joseph when his God-appointed identity was threatened and he experienced adversity. He was God's beloved son, God's appointed manager and dreamer, who would be bowed down to. Joseph spoke the truth of the dreams that God gave him, and he was hated by his brothers for it. He was hated for God's favor, for what God entrusted him with. He lived with integrity, even when those around him did not. Even as he bore the consequences of the identity God gave him, he never hid from who he was. He rose in the esteem of each of his overseers in every new circumstance that he found himself in because he was a trustworthy manager and leader. He lived out his identity as a born dreamer and interpreter of dreams. He faithfully endured what came his way.

Genesis 37:4–8 gives us the background: "But when his brothers saw that their father loved him more than all his brothers, they hated him and could not speak peacefully to him. Now Joseph had a dream, and when he told it to his brothers, they hated him even more. He said to them, 'Hear this dream that I have dreamed: Behold, we were binding sheaves in the field, and behold, my sheaf arose and stood upright. And behold, your sheaves gathered around it and bowed down to my sheaf.' His brothers said to him, 'Are you indeed to reign over us? Or are you indeed to rule over us?' So they hated him even more for his dreams and for his words." Joseph's brothers resent God's favor upon Joseph, and they mockingly call him a dreamer, denigrating one of the gifts of purpose that God had given Joseph. Shockingly, we see that Joseph's brothers hate him so much that they plot to kill him and settle for selling him into slavery (Genesis 37:28). Yet the Lord was with Joseph, His favor rested upon him, and he was successful in all he did and found favor with all of his masters. Genesis 39:2–4 says, "The Lord was with Joseph, and he became a successful man, and he was in the house of his Egyptian master. His master saw that the LORD was with him and that the LORD caused all that he did to succeed in his hands. So Joseph found favor in his sight and attended him, and he made him overseer of his house and put him in charge of all that he had."

The serpent did not let up but continued to attack the righteous actions of Joseph, now through the selfish actions of Potiphar's wife. She wanted him, but he honored Potiphar too much to dally with Potiphar's wife. She spread lies about him and he found himself in prison. Genesis 39:19–20 says, "As soon as his master heard the words that his wife spoke to him, 'This is the way your servant treated me,' his anger was kindled. And Joseph's master took him and put him into the prison." How awful! As if being a slave is not demeaning enough, now he is also a prisoner. What a far cry from his dream. Instead of others bowing to him, he would spend years bowing down to others. I could not imagine being able to stand firm in my identity as he did, enduring the amount of opposition that he faced. Never once do we see him falter or lose sight of his identity, and it was his identity that contributed to him becoming a slave. Oh, the grumblings and complaining that would have spewed from my lips in the same situation. *Ha. I'm a dreamer alright! I am delusional thinking anyone would bow down to me. See what doing the right thing gets you? My father sent me; in obedience I went and found myself unfairly stuffed in a pit and sold as a slave. When I face temptation, I do not succumb to it, but I still get accused of succumbing and become a prisoner.* From a worldly point of view, we might say, "How could things get worse?" Yet, Joseph continues serving God. Things, however, were not as bad as the situation implied, for the Lord was always with Joseph and showed him favor despite his circumstances. Genesis 39:21 says, "But the Lord was with Joseph and showed him steadfast love and gave him favor in the sight of the keeper of the prison."

When the time came for Joseph to stand out, he gave God the credit and took none upon himself. Genesis 41:15–16 says, "And Pharaoh said to Joseph, 'I have had a dream, and there is no one who can interpret it. I have heard it said of you that when you hear a dream you can interpret it.' Joseph answered Pharaoh, 'It is not in me; God will give Pharaoh a favorable answer.'" Joseph interpreted the dream and gave wise counsel to Pharaoh. Pharaoh saw the wisdom of Joseph and exalted him above all others in the land of Egypt. All that God allowed Joseph to endure was not to destroy his worth or to make him falter, but to allow him to step toward the identity and calling that God gave him, and as a result, his brothers bow before him. Genesis 42:6 says, "Now Joseph was governor over the land. He was the one who sold to all the people of the land. And Joseph's brothers came and bowed themselves before him with their faces to the ground."

Now Moses, by comparison, did not withstand the opposition and hardship. He buckled under the weight of his failure, and it affected him deeply. He fled from his past and did not want to revisit it. At this moment on Mount Horeb, he is still running and hiding. He ironically projects his own doubts about himself upon the Israelites, assuming they will not listen to the authority entrusted to him, when it is actually Moses, himself, who is not listening and believing the authority entrusted to him. For forty years, this calling of Moses has lain dormant, squelched from the fear and the failure that he experienced the last time he tried to live it out. The difference is that now it is in the power and timing of I AM.

Moses is not alone in doubting his identity, nor is fear the only way that our identity becomes warped. Adam and Eve were living their identity in perfection and things became distorted due to their pride. The serpent was willing to use Eve, to manipulate her, to get exactly what he wanted. This form of distortion and pride also has its way in our hearts. The serpent convinced them that they wanted more for themselves, and pride was born. Now, we all have become the focus and the recipient of our own identities. It is about me and for my benefit, and I manipulate and scheme to get what I want. But Jesus tells us in John 15:13, "Greater love has no one than this, that someone lay down his life for his friends." How often do we clutch at our possessions and our abilities because we do not want to lay down *our* identity for fear of that loss of identity rendering us empty, only to discover that clutched within our grasp is the death-striking serpent? Our true identity is found only when Jesus lives in us and through us and we are living that identity out for Him. Oh, does this speak to our need for a Savior. It points to our skewed perception of ourselves, of how we use what has been entrusted to us by God to further ourselves and to manipulate others to do what we want, convinced that we are good when our hearts are so deceived that we cannot even recognize it. We buy the lies that we define our purpose and our identity and that we have the right to pursue happiness at the expense of others. These are all ploys by the serpent to render us ineffective for God's kingdom work.

Let us consider how the Israelites needed to lay down the serpent, how they were relying on themselves instead of looking towards their Deliverer God. The time comes when the Israelites also must lay down the serpent. Exodus 14:8 says, "And the LORD hardened the heart of Pharaoh king of Egypt, and he pursued the people of Israel while the people of Israel were going out defiantly." They were riding high and feeling bold. We see obedience to God, but we do not see words of praise. They were walking out not only looking the part of victorious warriors but feeling like victorious warriors. Imagine with me the satisfaction and pride they must have felt to finally be free after so many years of slavery. The word *defiant* in this passage means "to lift up or exalt." Their boldness seems to be loftily focused on themselves, not directed towards God, who was delivering them.

Exodus 13:18 says, "But God led the people around by the way of the wilderness toward the Red Sea. And the people of Israel went up out of the land of Egypt equipped for battle." But when the Egyptians were bearing down on them, the truth that they are unable to save themselves quickly and resoundingly becomes apparent. They realize that they are not mighty warriors, but slaves disguised as warriors. Very quickly their prideful boldness dissipates with the realization that simply looking the part is not enough. They experience a different kind of fear than Moses, fear of failure at the cost of their very lives. Exodus 14:10 says, "When Pharaoh drew near, the people of Israel lifted up their eyes, and behold, the Egyptians were marching after them, and they feared greatly. And the people of Israel cried out to the LORD." This fear prevented them from seeing their identity. Their immediate thought was that they would perish. Exodus 14:11-12 describes their reaction: "They said to Moses, 'Is it because there are no graves in Egypt that you have taken us away to die in the wilderness? What have you done to us in bringing us out of Egypt? Is this not what we said to you in Egypt: 'Leave us alone that we may serve the Egyptians'? For it would have been better for us to serve the Egyptians than to die in the wilderness.'" They immediately revert and want to reassume their slave identity. The people of Israel, whose very name means "God prevails", forgot that it is God who prevails as they left defiantly and that God will prevail against this army pursuing them. They stopped being Israel, following truth under the direction and protection of God, and once again became a nation under Jacob, so shrouded in deceit and lies that they became immovable, petrified.

In an interview for a job, many of us have been asked the question, "What motivates you?" When asked this question, do you have to stop and think before you answer, or does it come readily off your tongue? Is there honesty in your answer, or do you say what would make you look good for the position? Have you ever been tempted to answer that question by listing your fears? Most of us would not be likely to correlate our fears to the behaviors that motivate us, but fear is often one of the biggest drivers in our lives. If we really stop and consider our actions, how often, like the Israelites, are we driven by our fears, over our dreams and our desires?

I can so clearly see this fear-based driver as I begin the book of Exodus. As I take in the actions of Pharaoh, whose title means "the great house of Egypt," I not only see a leader desiring power, but I just as clearly see a man ruled by the fear of losing that power. The great house of Egypt was afraid of the people of God's house because of their perceived ability to affect his power. He viewed them as a threat to his position. Pharaoh's actions, which were grounded in fear, seemed to be the beginning of his demise. As he started down this path, he became further and further invested in sinful, cruel, and violent behavior, and he brought his entire nation down with him. Through these fear-based actions, we discover that the great house of Egypt is no match for the house of God. All their plotting and maneuvering did not work, so they tried harder and harder and became more deeply entrenched in their sinful behavior. What began with scheming and plotting quickly moves to oppressing and mistreating and ends with the mass murder of innocents. We know that the hearts of the people always follow the heart of their king. Instead of shock and grief and loathing over the behavior and decisions of Pharaoh, the people of Egypt were sickened by and loathed the Israelites. *Lord God, my King, show me ways that I might be following other gods, how my heart is not following Your heart. How am I being ruled by fear instead of ruled by my desire to bring honor and glory to Your name? How am I sickened by and how do I loathe Your ways instead of being sickened by and loathing the wickedness of the world?*

The irony in this story is that the one with the power was the one who was ruled by fear. The powerless slave midwives were fearless and acted boldly and courageously, and the mighty leader driven by fear acted like a coward. When we compare Pharaoh's behavior to that of the midwives, we see the one with the power plotting and scheming to retain it and women without any control whatsoever, except for the power of choice, resting in the Lord. If asked in an interview what motivates them, their response would have been, without hesitation, "obeying the Lord." They feared God and desired to please Him more than they feared Pharaoh. The value and worth of these women were crafted by the hands of God and they recognized that. Their purposes were imagined and developed for them by God. Before their birth, God designed them and created their identities to be splendid helpers to bring forth life. What a beautiful God-given purpose. What does Satan try to force on them through Pharaoh? An ugly distortion of truth. Pharaoh, as a pawn for Satan, tried to force them to become life takers, women who were horrific and unfair. But these women held firm to the truth of who they were, the truth of who God created them to be. When you are known by God, you know your purpose and you walk in that purpose. As Jesus said in John 10:27, "My sheep hear my voice, and I know them, and they follow me."

God has shown me how I do not trust every step on His path, even though I was convinced that I trust His perfect plan. The fear of being consumed by evil grips me. I stand in terror in the big moments, moments like this, when God asked Moses to go back from where he fled, back to where he did not belong. I also struggle to continue along a path that God has called me to if that path requires me to remain faithfully reliant on Him. I want every storm to be mild and to leave quickly. I would have wanted to take the quickest route to the Promised Land, regardless of what I needed to learn in the wilderness. But God does nothing randomly. There is purpose in each action He takes.

Do you ever read something in the Bible and just get giddy from its significance? One such thing for me is Exodus 3:12, "He said, 'But I will be with you, and this shall be the sign for you, that I have sent you: when you have brought the people out of Egypt, you shall serve God on this mountain.'" Why would Moses need confirmation that he was sent by God after the people were successfully freed from bondage and the Egyptian army destroyed? Signs usually precede the event the sign is intended for. This sign takes place after deliverance. Why would Moses need a sign of being sent after the deliverance was completed, after he ventured into Egypt to fulfill this purpose? It struck me that this is not a sign for the "big" moment of deliverance. This is not intended to give him courage to go to Egypt. This is a sign during the wait in the wilderness. The very first sign God gives Moses is a reassurance to stay the course when he is leading God's sheep, when things are hard and people are grumbling and dissatisfied, and when it seems like nothing is happening. It is a reminder to him that God is with him and has chosen him. This is encouragement to be patient, to trust in God's goodness in the waiting, after the high of the big moment of deliverance has waned, when you begin to feel weary and doubt takes root.

I see a new glimpse of my God in relation to His path and His plan. This is a God who continually reveals Himself and affirms to us that we can trust Him. I see a God who is preparing us for the next leg of the journey before this leg of the journey even begins because His plan is that solid and trustworthy. His plan is already laid out even when we do not see it. He does not need to scheme and maneuver, trying to figure it out as He goes. He knows and moves to complete His will. While convincing Moses to go to Egypt, He is already preparing him for the time subsequent to the deliverance. He is laying the groundwork for Moses to not doubt His perfect, sovereign plan during the wait, and, when Moses finally lays down the serpent, he will discover that neither his imperfections nor the grumbling and complaining of the Israelites can stop the plans of God.

Many of us begin adulthood with grand plans. We have splendid hopes of how our lives are going to turn out and a collection of ideas of how to make it happen. Even with the best and most encouraging of parents, we venture out with thoughts of the "right" way of doing things, determined to make our mark in the world because there are some things that the previous generation just does not understand. In our minds, we have constructed a course that will lead us not only to, but through, lush, plentiful gardens where everything works itself out. If we try hard enough, success is ours for the taking with minimal hiccups and no derailments along the way. Life, however, tends to present a vast wilderness without clearly defined direction, instead of the marked path within the garden of plenty that we anticipated. We discover that life is not easy. We face rejection, betrayal, and hurt. We battle health issues and loss. We experience financial pressures. We begin prioritizing going through the motions of what must be done over that which brings breath to our lungs. When these stresses and challenges of life happen, the optimism and enthusiasm of youth erode. We turn from our dreams and our calling because we are battling every day to get by. We become embittered, jaded, and worn, and we tend to begin settling for a life that does not come close to mirroring the ideals we once held. By letting go of these ideals and giving up the fight, we discover a complacent contentment, not quite the territory of an abundant life but vastly superior to the disappointment of fighting for, and never receiving, what our hearts truly desire.

My adult life has followed this course. I was so optimistic and expectant of happiness, but my life has been marked with confusion and loneliness for years, which has driven me to withdraw from people. Thinking that I had life all figured out may have initially helped to direct my path, but it also added to my disappointment along the way. It highlighted how far I was from what I wanted to achieve. I was not looking for fame or glory, but within my quiet spirit that always waited to be acknowledged and invited was a longing to belong and to lead, only my personality did not lend itself to being followed. My twenties were marked by pleasing everyone. The more I felt different from those around me, the more I hid parts of myself that were different. Despite major accomplishments which validated to me that I controlled the path I was on, like getting a college degree and getting married, I quickly discovered that the world was not mine to control. No matter how hard I tried to belong and please the people around me, it did not actually enable me to control their pleasure. Instead, my inability to consistently please devoured my pleasure and allowed others to control me. I recognized that the life that I had built around others was easily broken. Trying to keep this fragile life from shattering around me was wearying and consumed all my energy. There was no rest. Despite the appearance of success, it was a time marked with sadness, confusion, and disillusionment. It seemed that I got what I wanted, yet I lacked life. I was like a bowl of fake fruit or artificial flowers that looked shiny and appealing but had no life, no substance, and no nutrients.

Even before my marriage began, I sensed things were extremely fragile. I focused all my attention on trying to hold together what I had built. I hid so many parts of myself to be accepted that I no longer recognized what I stood for. I tried to become everything that I thought my husband wanted me to be, and it still was not enough. When you have invested everything in your life in belonging to one person, and that person no longer wants you, you are shredded. You feel chewed up and spit out. Amid all my broken pieces came the recognition of just how hollow my life was. Even the shadow of my personality, the appealing, perfect parts, what I allowed someone to see, was not enough to make me belong. I was cast aside and rejected. In a situation like this, what you've spent years building is shattered in an instant. The belief that you have built your life upon, that you can accomplish anything if you just try hard enough, is exposed as shifting sand, a vicious lie that will not support you. Giving everything to something or someone is just not enough. Suddenly, your entire world drops out from underneath you and you fall.

But people are resilient. We learn to adjust. Like Moses, I felt like I started again from nothing, rebuilding my life. I moved on. I remarried. The lesson I took with me, from my experience, was that, if the selfish and the bold succeed, and the meek and the giving pay, I must never put myself in the position of being the giving one or being meek again. I must try less for others and do what I want. I was determined to never again be driven by what someone else wanted me to be. I became bolder in laying claim to who I wanted to be and less concerned about the needs of others. The problem is, I am not naturally bold. I am not someone who demands what she wants. I am a pleaser by nature. It is in the fabric of my DNA, so unknowingly, I began battling myself. There is an innate part of me that derives pleasure from pleasing the people that I love. So, the more I tried to go after what I wanted, the more bitter I became. I was angry when I did not get what I wanted, guilty when I fought for and got my way, and frustrated that I was not satisfied with any of it. I became someone that I did not recognize, always angry and bitter, always looking for someone to blame. I was constantly under a self-created, intense pressure to be perfect, ready to implode.

To add to the upheaval, confusion, and anger, while I went after what I wanted, something deep within kept resurfacing no matter how much I tried to squash it down. My barometer to gauge my success was the feedback that I received from others. If someone commended me, I would ride so high. If someone criticized me, I was in the lowest low. So, while I was not actively seeking to please others, I was still bound by what others thought. The irony of it all is that my method of protecting myself from getting hurt was more hurtful to me because I was still seeking the validation of others to affirm my worth, even if I was not actively seeking to please them, so I doomed myself to failure. I constantly failed in my own mind by accomplishing what I was determined I was no longer going to do.

I continued to hide not only my weaknesses but who I really was from people. I was still consumed with not failing, constantly striving for perfection. No longer was I goaded into being someone else by their criticism; now I was trapping myself into being someone that I am not in order to prevent being hurt again. I would berate myself for not being bold and courageous. I would criticize myself for being weak and needing validation from others. There was no denigration that I could receive from others that came close to matching the abuse I heaped on myself. I traded in my artificial fruit for something that seemed more alive but turned out to be nothing but weeds that were choking the life out of me.

My life became a constant reminder that I could not live up to my own standard of perfection. It was exhausting to simultaneously go after what I wanted, hide my imperfections, and try to gain everyone's approval. It was as if I was trying to go in all directions at once, expending a great deal of energy getting nowhere. This constant reminder that I could not do it all, that I was failing over and over, drove me to absolute rage. I would look for people or things that I could blame. Initially, it was always someone else's fault. My husband was the easiest target. In my rage, it was so easy to convince myself and to blame my partner for not doing his share and causing my mess. Then the recognition of the real reason for my wrath, my inability to control everything perfectly, would surface. The recognition of my own shortcomings, coupled with the guilt of speaking ill of someone, would plague me, so my wrath would turn inwards. I would attack myself in unhealthy ways, brutally dissecting everything I said and did, obsessing over how I should have done it differently or better. I was exhausted from constantly not being enough and from finding myself lacking in every aspect of my life.

Then God called me by name, calling me from the wilderness, from this communityless, unengaged life I was leading without His abundance. He called me to community. Like Moses, I wanted to throw out every reason why I did not want to be sent back into the land of "community." Even though I was not satisfied, there was a level of comfort for me in being alone in the wilderness. But, also like Moses, God continues to address every fear and every excuse one by one.

I was obedient, but it was not easy. I did not immediately make connections. Things did not quickly and easily fall into place. God slowly began surrounding me with women who loved Him deeply. They were women who modeled how to serve others well, and, just like I recognize the self-absorption of Moses in this passage of Exodus, there came a moment where I realized that all my fears of not belonging and of failing stemmed from being predominantly focused on myself, which prevented me from seeing others. I had little concern for the struggles people were enduring or whether they were under the burden of sin. As I laid down the solitary "I-do-not-need-community" outlook, God showed me my identity's serpent. I came to the realization that all the effort I put forth to please others was really a manipulative way for me to validate myself.

As I watched these fruit-bearing women and recognized their authentic hearts reaching out to others because they genuinely cared for them, I asked God to develop a heart like that within me. As I worked on trying to have a heart of love and joy, of focusing on others above myself, I failed daily. It was a time of frustration and of humbling, a time when my heart was being tilled and softened. God was bringing me to the end of myself because, in my own power, I could not be the person He calls me to be. I began to understand His never-ending mercy to a greater depth. I discovered that the more I began to recognize God's mercy and compassion towards me, the more mercy and compassion I began to extend to others. The grace of God was taking root more deeply into my heart, which allowed me to extend grace further out.

~

PAUSE TO PRAISE AND PONDER:

Theme: Letting go of how we view ourselves to live according to how God made us.
Read Exodus 4:1–4.

Brainstorming:
When have you experienced God leading you to let go of something? Is God currently leading you to let go of something?
How has God led you back to a very similar situation? How have the results differed?
What situation has wounded you deeply?
What situations have embarrassed you?
What situations have caused you guilt and shame?
What are you drawn toward but hesitant to pursue?

Get Creative:
- Reflect on the lies that might be lurking within. Draw a serpent. In the space around the serpent, write different aspects of your personality, your identity, and how you are or may be called by name. Inside the serpent, write ways that you live your identity outside of God's purposes in fear, hiding, doubt, or a desire for comfort for yourself.

Daily Bread: In what ways can you bring God praise? How is God personally calling you? What word, phrase, action, or topic is He revealing to you?

- Draw a drinking glass. Select a verse related to what God has revealed to you today as you pondered that speaks truth about the ways and promises of God.
- Draw a sandwich.
    - On the bottom bun, praise God by writing how you know that God created you uniquely for His specific purpose.

- Select one way that you use your identity for your own purposes outside of God's purpose.
- On the top bun, write a truth contained in God's Word that speaks about the blessing of living out your purpose and identity in God.

6

CATCHING THE SERPENT BY THE TAIL

Exodus 4:2-4 "*The* LORD *said to him, 'What is that in your hand?' He said, 'A staff.' And he said, 'Throw it on the ground.' So he threw it on the ground, and it became a serpent, and Moses ran from it. But the* LORD *said to Moses, 'Put out your hand and catch it by the tail'—so he put out his hand and caught it, and it became a staff in his hand.*"

My daughter was born for the water. Every chance she gets, she will swim for hours. Even when the waters of Lake Erie are freezing, you will find her the lone swimmer, with goose bumps all over her body, frolicking and playing until her lips turn purple. All summer long her favorite place is the water of the lake. During the winter, as the water becomes too cold, she is forced to go indoors to swim. But indoor swimming comes with more rules. To ensure safety, children are only allowed in certain areas of the pool if they pass a swimming test. Kids with access to the deep areas wear a green armband; those who have not passed wear a red one. One day, as we were playing in the water, I watched my daughter swim half of the length of the pool with ease. I realized that she was ready. I encouraged her to try to take the test, but she hesitated. "What if I fail?" As her mother, not wanting to see her fail out of fear, I encouraged her to step forward despite her fear. I explained that I would not encourage her to try something if I did not think that she was ready for it. Because I do not always walk my talk, I intimately know from experience that not doing something from fear of failing is failing already. Do it often enough and it deeply affects you. Each time it reinforces to you just a little bit more how very weak you are. Life becomes sideline living, watching others attempt while you safely exist. Not taking the test and not passing the test result in the same outcome: no access to certain areas of the pool. I explained it all to her. She responded, "I don't want to fail in front of all these people." Fear of how she might look in front of others won this day. Extending patience that I really do not possess, I dropped the subject, letting her know that the subject was not permanently dropped but temporarily laid aside and that I would be bringing it up every time we went swimming.

She spent that night over at a friend's house, and they went swimming again the next day. Because she was forced to remain in the shallower water, while her friend was afforded the luxury of freedom anywhere within the pool, her friend finally convinced her to try. She passed all parts of the swim test on the first try, although she had three tries for each part. She returned home with her hand covering her wrist and said, "Mom, look!" As she moved her hand away, with pride she showed me her green wristband, and I was so happy for her. I knew she could do it. As her parent, while I could not guarantee her success, I believed in her ability. I am her biggest supporter. I will be behind her encouraging as long as God gives us both air to breathe. God not only supports us but He guarantees our success. But, like my daughter, Moses was so focused on the lies he believed, like, "I don't want to fail in front of all these people," that he could not recognize God's encouragement and support of truth guaranteeing his success. God does not give up. He relentlessly pursues us. He does not allow Moses to fail by not going. He continues to encourage and show Moses that He will be with him until Moses relents and follows Him.

As if the staff becoming a serpent was not odd enough, one of the most confusing events occurs after Moses lays down the staff. God tells Moses to pick it back up. Have you ever laid something down for God and He asks you to pick it back up? Have you ever wrestled for years to let go of your desires to yield them to God, only to have God ask you what you desire? Your first inclination is to profusely shake your head, denying His request. When we finally come to the end of ourselves and lay our desires down, the last thing we want to do is pick them back up. We finally recognize the serpent within us. We understand it for what it is. We have felt its venom coursing through us, robbing us of life. We know its deadly venom and run from it as Moses runs from the serpent in self-preservation—the only time, since fleeing Egypt, that we ever see Moses flee. Take in, however, what happens when the serpent is picked back up. The staff which revealed itself as a serpent, which represents Moses's identity, all that he has to offer, once again becomes a staff, but this is no ordinary staff. It is now a transformed instrument of God, full of His authority and power. It is a new staff, rid of the deceit tainting it, ready to be used for God's purposes. From turning the Nile to blood to bringing forth the plagues of frogs and locusts to crossing the Red Sea, Moses uses this transformed staff to perform almost every miracle within the land of Egypt and beyond into the wilderness as he leads these people.

God tells Moses that this is one of the signs that he can use so the Israelites will believe him (Exodus 4:8–9), but the people are not the only ones who need help to believe. Moses needs to be convinced that the power and might of God is enough. How amazing that what God provides to the people so they will believe Moses also serves as a constant reminder to Moses! This staff is always in his hand. Moses is unable to do these things on his own, but with God, nothing is impossible. It is God who changes our feeble attempts and our failures. It is God who converts our actions to prosperity, and it is God who holds the victory. Then, we see transformation displayed again in the next miracle God shows Moses as his hand full of leprosy is restored (Exodus 4:6–7). This miracle echoes the truth we find in Exodus 15:26, "If you will diligently listen to the voice of the Lord your God, and do that which is right in his eyes, and give ear to his commandments and keep all his statutes, I will put none of the diseases on you that I put on the Egyptians, for I am the Lord, your healer." God takes what is sick and broken and transforms it. He is not satisfied with deliverance alone. God reveals His transformative nature in the wilderness but personally teaches it to Moses in this moment.

Yet, despite all that God shows him, Moses prefers to keep his life of tending sheep. Exodus 4:13 says, "But he said, 'Oh, my Lord, please send someone else.'" I wonder what was going through Moses's mind here. Is his doubt so strong, is the distortion of his abilities so severe, that he cannot envision the truth of what God is saying? Is he now so comfortable with this new life that he does not want to revisit the past full of slavery and oppression? Whatever drove him to utter this request, one thing we do know is that his heart is predominantly, if not solely, focused inward. His statements reveal that he neither focused on God's words, nor on all those people who are suffering and needy. Yet God graciously continues to give. Despite the marvelous promises of God, none of God's answers convince Moses to willingly go, so God graciously gives Moses his brother Aaron to speak to the people on his behalf, even though God, the maker of Moses's mouth, was more than enough for him to complete the task (Exodus 4:10–16). What a merciful God to not give up on us in our selfishness and fear! What a gracious God to provide beyond what we need, even when grievous doubt about His sovereignty exists in our hearts!

Finally, after this promise, Moses goes to his father-in-law, Jethro, requesting that he be allowed to go back to his people. How often do we rely on the support of man before we comply with the requests of God? Within this moment, Moses shows deference to Jethro, recognizing him as an authority by asking his permission. The fascinating thing to note about this request is that it is not entirely truthful. It is as if Moses is still hiding, even in this land so far from Egypt. Is he trying to hide what he is convinced will be failure from his father-in-law? Exodus 4:18 tells us, "Moses went back to Jethro his father-in-law and said to him, 'Please let me go back to my brothers in Egypt to see whether they are still alive.'" What an interesting, complex character that Moses is. By appearances, it seems that Moses shows more deference to Jethro than to God by asking Jethro's permission when he debates with God over God's calling on his life. Yet, Moses withholds and hides from Jethro, while he is authentic and real with God. There is something poignant and beautiful in that discovery. Even when we hide our weaknesses and failures before man, we do not need to fear being authentic and raw with God.

Before Moses enters Egypt, God sends Aaron out to meet Moses. As Aaron shares the words of the Lord and performs the mighty acts that God showed Moses, the people believe. There are joy and worship. Exodus 4:31 says, "And the people believed; and when they heard that the LORD had visited the people of Israel and that he had seen their affliction, they bowed their heads and worshipped." Moses's fears were not realized. The difference between similar situations when God is involved is amazing. When he took matters into his own hands, Moses was accused of butting in, making himself their prince and judge, and it caused Moses to flee from Pharaoh. Now as he is performing God's will, in God's timing, the people of Israel believe him, and he begins his appointed role as the one who will bring God's deliverance to these people. He stands before Pharaoh face-to-face, fulfilling the role of Israel's leader and their judge, under the direction of God.

Cannot you just imagine God saying to Moses, "Moses, it is not you but me they do not believe. I will bring deliverance, but, first, I need you to trust me, to wait on me." The increased oppression at the hands of the Egyptians makes the deliverance even more obvious and even sweeter. It leaves no doubt that deliverance belongs to God, not Moses.

But Moses quickly discovers, however, that things can be worse than even he imagined. All his fears were focused on himself. Never once, in all his hesitation, did he ever consider the impact on God's people. After he speaks to Pharaoh, the horrible treatment of God's people intensifies. Their burden is not relieved but made worse. For Moses, what would be worse than not being believed? Being believed, giving hope, and watching those hopes and dreams crushed beneath the weight of such oppression. Exodus 6:9 says, "Moses spoke thus to the people of Israel, but they did not listen to Moses, because of their broken spirit and harsh slavery." For the first time in Moses's conversation with God, we see concern for the people on Moses's lips, not just concern for himself. Exodus 5:22–23 shows this concern in Moses's reaction after the Egyptians intensify the suffering of the Israelites: "Then Moses turned to the LORD and said, 'O Lord, why have you done evil to this people? Why did you ever send me? For since I came to Pharaoh to speak in your name, he has done evil to this people, and you have not delivered your people at all.'"

Moses still has so much to learn about I AM, about His sovereignty, His power, and His authority. Under the tutelage of God's patient wisdom, we see Moses's compassion growing for God's people, an important element in shepherding them. As time goes on, we see Moses growing into the man God made him to be. We see him step forward in faith. We see his belief in God solidify. We see him speak truth to Jethro, and we see how his testimony solidifies Jethro's faith in the one true God. Exodus 18:8–12 tells us,

"Then Moses told his father-in-law all that the LORD had done to Pharaoh and to the Egyptians for Israel's sake, all the hardship that had come upon them in the way, and how the LORD had delivered them. And Jethro rejoiced for all the good that the LORD had done to Israel, in that he had delivered them out of the hand of the Egyptians. Jethro said, 'Blessed be the LORD, who has delivered you out of the hand of the Egyptians and out of the hand of Pharaoh and has delivered the people from under the hand of the Egyptians. Now I know that the LORD is greater than all gods, because in this affair they dealt arrogantly with the people.' And Jethro, Moses' father-in-law, brought a burnt offering and sacrifices to God; and Aaron came with all the elders of Israel to eat bread with Moses' father-in-law before God." Somewhere between being called by name and doing God's will, Moses comes to know a steadfast, loving God who can be relied upon, and the transformation this brings to his life is astounding. He lays down his concern for himself and carries out God's will with concern for God's people. Moses becomes a man who intercedes for God's people out of concern for them over concern for himself.

Amazingly, what we discover about God's sovereign plan is that even as Moses's life veered off course, Moses was never outside of God's plans for him. Even when Moses was tucked away, hiding in the wilderness, God was working. During this time of tending sheep, God was familiarizing him with the wilderness. He was preparing Moses to tend to His flock. He was equipping Moses for the final forty years of his life as the shepherd of God's people in the wilderness. This is what being known by God is all about. It does not matter what has happened to you before. Past failures and past sins do not prevent your service to God, nor do they define you. It does not matter how long you have been hiding in fear or complacency. God ensures that you will bear fruit in season. Psalm 1:3 says about the righteous person, "He is like a tree planted by streams of water that yields its fruit in its season, and its leaf does not wither. In all that he does, he prospers."

Through it all, God was equipping Moses. We receive yet another mind-blowing paradox: that God equips us even though God is all we ever really need. All the equipment in the world is lacking if God's power and authority are not moving in our midst. Without God, the staff of Moses is nothing but a stick. God's power and authority will prevail even when we are not equipped at all. Abraham could not, in his own power, bring his son back to life, yet he was willing to sacrifice Isaac because he knew that God promised that he would father many nations and that Isaac was the promised child. Genesis 22:12 describes the result: "He said, 'Do not lay your hand on the boy or do anything to him, for now I know that you fear God, seeing you have not withheld your son, your only son, from me.'" The sheep follow the voice of their Shepherd. They are secure in the knowledge that He knows them and that they have a place with the Shepherd. The sheep know they can trust their Shepherd, even in moments where they are relinquishing something or someone dear to them.

The Israelites left Egypt equipped for battle, yet they did not fight at all. God fought for them. Moses predicts this in Exodus 14:13-14: "And Moses said to the people, "Fear not, stand firm, and see the salvation of the LORD, which he will work for you today. For the Egyptians whom you see today, you shall never see again. The LORD will fight for you, and you have only to be silent." It is the staff of God that Moses uses to part the waters of the Red Sea, as described in Exodus 14:15-16: "The LORD said to Moses, "Why do you cry to me? Tell the people of Israel to go forward. Lift up your staff, and stretch out your hand over the sea and divide it, that the people of Israel may go through the sea on dry ground." It is God who puts Himself in between the Israelites and the Egyptians, as described in Exodus 14:19-20: "Then the angel of God who was going before the host of Israel moved and went behind them, and the pillar of cloud moved from before them and stood behind them, coming between the host of Egypt and the host of Israel. And there was the cloud and the darkness. And it lit up the night without one coming near the other all night." It was God who defeated the Egyptians. Exodus 14:23–31 describes this victory in full: "The Egyptians pursued and went in after them into the midst of the sea, all Pharaoh's horses, his chariots, and his horsemen. And in the morning watch the LORD in the pillar of fire and of cloud looked down on the Egyptian forces and threw the Egyptian forces into a panic, clogging their chariot wheels so that they drove heavily. And the Egyptians said, 'Let us flee from before Israel, for the LORD fights for them against the Egyptians.' Then the LORD said to Moses, 'Stretch out your hand over the sea, that the water may come back upon the Egyptians, upon their chariots, and upon their horsemen.' So Moses stretched out his hand over the sea, and the sea returned to its normal course when the morning appeared. And as the Egyptians fled into it, the LORD threw the Egyptians into the midst of the sea. The waters returned and covered the chariots and the horsemen; of all the host of Pharaoh that had followed them into the sea, not one of them remained. But the people of Israel walked on dry ground through the sea, the waters being a wall to them on their right hand and on their left. Thus the LORD saved Israel that day from the hand of the Egyptians, and Israel saw the Egyptians dead on the seashore. Israel saw the great power that the LORD used against the Egyptians, so the people feared the LORD, and they believed in the LORD and in his servant Moses."

Exodus 14:13 tells us, "And Moses said to the people, 'Fear not, stand firm, and see the salvation of the LORD, which he will work for you today. For the Egyptians whom you see today, you shall never see again.'" Finally, they come to understand that God is their Mighty Warrior, and knowing that God fights for them is what makes them become God's mighty warriors. They declare in Exodus 15:2: "The LORD is my strength and my song, and he has become my salvation; this is my God, and I will praise him, my father's God, and I will exalt him." The Israelites find themselves in a place where there is nothing left for them to do but to worship and praise God. He has handled everything for them. They silently watch Him act with a mighty hand.

The realization that all our talents and abilities do not affect God's ability to complete His plan could mire us down in uselessness and worthlessness. Why bother if God completes it all anyways? But it has the opposite effect. All our inability, frailty, failure, and weakness no longer matter. We step into the light knowing the only equipping needed is God Himself, with us, fighting for us. All I need is Jesus living in me and through me. There is something so freeing in knowing that my heart longing to please Him is enough to delight Him, even when my execution falls so short. Like children who do things without expertise but enthusiastically try to garner the praise of their parents, God does not expect us to live up to some standard of perfection. Our doing brings Him delight. I think of my children and my focus on doing everything right. Oh, to rewind time and let them spill the milk on the floor as they fill their own glasses, to be patient and allow them to try, to allow them to do things slowly and inefficiently as God does with us! Why was I in such a hurry? Why did I strive so hard for perfection? God teaches us His cadence, "You are because I AM. I AM enough."

My initial thought towards the Israelites as they wander the desert is that they are very dramatic, mistrustful people. They immediately go to doubt and ingratitude, and it seems so extreme. This attitude is demonstrated in Exodus 16:3–4: "And the people of Israel said to them, 'Would that we had died by the hand of the LORD in the land of Egypt, when we sat by the meat pots and ate bread to the full, for you have brought us out into this wilderness to kill this whole assembly with hunger.' Then the LORD said to Moses, 'Behold, I am about to rain bread from heaven for you, and the people shall go out and gather a day's portion every day, that I may test them, whether they will walk in my law or not.'" But then I slow down my critique and I consider, *Is there more to their complaints than tirelessly voicing their unmet expectations? Were the pots of meat and the bread the only things that Israel had to fill themselves with in their years in captivity? Their one and only luxury? As their dignity, freedom, and children were taken from them, was this food all that they had to hold on to during those bleak times? Was the lack of water and food in the wilderness representative of the smidgen of comfort that they had in Egypt being taken away? Did it leave them feeling even more out of control because even the meager things they could rely on were removed and now they find themselves empty-handed in the desert?* Now suddenly, when I could not relate to their situation and frowned upon their behavior, now I find myself empathizing and understanding them a little bit more. When I consider their trauma and life experiences, I realize how difficult it is to let go of traumatic events, and I discover a compassion for them and their fears. Of course they have difficulty trusting. Look at what the powerful god king who ruled over them inflicted upon them. They have every reason to be mistrustful and jaded, but God is patiently teaching them that He is no ordinary King. He is trustworthy. As God tests the Israelites, His purpose is to teach them their true identities. He is teaching them the way of abundance, not leading them to death as they fear. They are made to be filled with God's law, not the oppressor's meat and bread. They are God's faith walkers, not Egypt's belly-stuffing sitters. God's goodness focuses on and is concerned with how we walk with Him, not in ensuring that we sit in plenty and comfort. It leads me to ask the question, In what ways am I so riddled with concern over my own comfort, my safety, or my success that I miss walking with God? How do I so quickly forget His marvelous ways and actions because I focus on the next problem before me?

We discover that the Israelites are warriors of God, but they fight only after they realize that it is God who wins the battle for them. We see an example of this in Exodus 17:9-11, "So Moses said to Joshua, 'Choose for us men, and go out and fight with Amalek. Tomorrow I will stand on top of the hill with the staff of God in my hand. So Joshua did as Moses told him, and fought with Amalek, while Moses, Aaron, and Hur went up to the top of the hill. Whenever Moses held up his hand, Israel prevailed, and whenever he lowered his hand, Amalek prevailed." It is the authority of God, within the staff of Moses, winning the battle. Not these men. Not Joshua. Exodus 17:13 describes the conclusion to the battle, "And Joshua overwhelmed Amalek and his people with the sword." The Israelites become the warriors that they portrayed as they left Egypt defiantly. They fight the Amalekites, yet it is the staff of God which wins the battle. The men on the battlefield do not win the battle, although God sends them to the battlefield and uses them on it. God continues to send us to the battlefield and uses us on the battlefield, but it is God who wins the battle. God desires for them, and us, to see and understand that He prevails for His people.

It is not only God's chosen people who will complete what God has purposed on His behalf. The hardened heart that does not listen, see, or act in obedience to God and the soft heart that does just as the Lord commands both fulfill that which is purposed by God. He is so wholly sovereign that He uses every heart to fulfill his purposes. His words, His works, and His ways cannot be challenged. He has no rival. As I Am, the thoughts, plans, and words of God will be fulfilled. Every single person will take part in fulfilling the grand purposes of God, whether by submitting or defying. God uses the actions of Pharaoh because God knows. He tells Moses and Aaron exactly how Pharaoh is going to react, and God uses this hard, unyielding heart as much as he uses Moses's soft, compassionate heart to deliver His chosen people. As God says in Exodus 7:4, "'I will lay my hand on Egypt and bring my hosts, my people the children of Israel, out of the land of Egypt.'"

Astoundingly, Moses never tries to hide his heart from God. He speaks about his reservations, his fears, and his desires in authenticity. God does not strike him down or punish him. God sends him anyways. It is not until God walks side by side with him and speaks to him face to face, teaching him to fulfill the purposes that God created for him, that Moses finally understands who God made him to be. When Moses becomes who God made him to be, it is as if we no longer see Moses at all. We see Jesus in Moses! Our identity is not for our own pleasure. There is no greater joy than living out who God made us to be! We speak of grace and how the perfection of Jesus covers us, but often our hearts have not grasped the full measure of that grace, which will never leave or ever fail us. We cannot give away what we do not possess. How can we speak of the joy of following Christ, while our hearts are filled with obligation to serve Him instead of living the joy of walking with Him? He must teach us the joy of knowing Him, a joy that is only fully understood when we realize that God continually draws near and forgives no matter how many times we fail. It is a joy born from discovering that we will fail to continually live in a manner worthy of Him, yet we will never fail to live out and accomplish what He has purposed for us to do. The danger of skipping past understanding that we are known by God is that we tend to try and hide our imperfections and our failures. So, when we venture out as salt and light, we expect perfection from ourselves and do not allow grace to work in us, so it can work through us.

Whenever I read passages addressing dying to self or decreasing so Jesus would increase, I always thought letting go of self meant letting go of what makes you, you: who you are and what you like. Remember, I am used to shadow living—trying to be what you think you ought to be, not who you were made to be. It is draining, not life-giving, always being on high alert, trying to hide the cracks in your armor. Can you comprehend my delight when I understood that laying down our lives is more about who we are living for than it is about a cessation of being ourselves? It is with an exhale of held breath that I realize that I do not have to be an exuberant extrovert who strikes up and carries a conversation with everyone I come across. Rather, laying down my life is a shift of the mind and heart. It is turning from selfish living and prideful demands for our own desires and our own gain. It is following, yielding to, and living for Jesus that may require, at times, exuberantly striking up a conversation in obedience. But, most importantly, the result is that when people look at us, they see the love of Jesus aimed towards them. We glow with his glory and righteousness because we have been transformed by his love and grace like Moses was transformed.

God knows you and He made you for a specific purpose. If He is with you and what you are doing is for His name, you cannot fail. Let go of the lies, the deceit, the doubt, and the discouragement. Lay down any manipulative tactics or deceit wrapped up in your identity. Check your heart. Who are you doing this for? Yourself? Others? God? Lay down your identity for Jesus as He laid down His life for you. If you are not acting for Him, there is only frustration. There is no prosperity, only a serpent's version of the truth, which is a vicious trap. As Moses will later realize, our identity is found in God alone. The possession of the Promised Land is useless if God is not among them. Moses recognized this in Exodus 33:15–16: "And he said to him, 'If your presence will not go with me, do not bring us up from here. For how shall it be known that I have found favor in your sight, I and your people? Is it not in your going with us, so that we are distinct, I and your people, from every other people on the face of the earth?'" It was no longer about success or failure or whether he would be believed. It was about God being in their midst. Moses comes to understand that it is God alone that defines and sets apart this group of people.

As a facilitator of a summer Bible study, instead of asking the large group to go around introduce themselves, which would have likely resulted in so many answers of what we do instead of who we are, I asked the ladies of this group to share one word to describe who God uniquely made them to be. I could hear the collective groan around the room, and I could see the discomfort that I was asking them to do this, but as we began there were so many lovely, uplifting answers. It was by far my favorite "introduction" to a Bible study I've ever been a part of. If you were limited to so few words, how would you describe yourself to those around you? It forces you to be succinct and focus on only the really important details. I settled for something that gives a little detail about me but skimmed the surface of who I really am.

Recently, I was tasked with providing a bio. In seventy words, I had to describe myself. Why is this something that makes us groan? We hate having to analyze ourselves in this way and usually run to someone we trust to help us objectively see ourselves. All too often we answer by describing what we do instead of giving information about who we are. It caused me to take a hard look at the question, What exactly makes me, me? Am I an accumulation of my name, family, and occupation rounded out by what I like, maybe sprinkled with what I have accomplished? I ended up loving this exercise, and this bio laid some of the groundwork for this book because it was so difficult for me to answer the question, "Who am I?"

If I go beyond the surface, I am a dreamer who possesses a relentless mind. I am a ponderer who tends to hyperfocus. I am wired to analyze, critique, and assess, so I am a natural problem solver. While these traits make me good at my job, I tend to obsess over things in a negative, unhealthy manner. God began breaking down the lies of my identity and replacing them with truth. He has revealed to me that my nature to please, which has caused me such turmoil and harm, is a beautiful picture of our Christ who longs to extend favor and delight to His people. When I seek God's will, when I see people and reach out to them with a heart that is focused outward and not focused on myself, the need to be seen, accepted, or perfect disappears. I am secure in being known and accepted by God, and I long to make others feel seen and accepted. My heart is beyond full—it is overflowing—and I get a glimpse of the person that God created me to be. I was made to see and to accept. When I can switch away from Satan's attack of convincing me to focus on myself and how I do not fit in, I focus on others, and God allows me to see them. Instead of my heart refusing to step toward the calling God has planned for me and reacting similarly to Moses in Exodus 3:13, "*Oh, my Lord, please send someone else,*" it is with excitement that I ask God to prepare my heart and to give me courage to step into the plans that He has for me. The unseen girl without a voice speaks and writes about the very things that she used to hide to help others understand how God transforms lives. Oh, she had to reach down and pick the serpent up by the tail, only to discover that all those things that she felt made her imperfect and unworthy of serving her perfect God are exactly what He uses to move His Kingdom forward. All those years of being unseen have given me a heart that desires to see others who are unseen. All those times when I felt so very different from the world because I crave depth over surface have driven me to commune with God by pondering His Word. I have lived the command found in Joshua 1:8, "This Book of the Law shall not depart from your mouth, but you shall meditate on it day and night, so that you may be careful to do according to all that is written in it. For then you will make your way prosperous, and then you will have good success." This life has allowed me to discover God's depths and understand how He knows me, and now He allows me to proclaim that to the world. I have learned that giving away produces and holding onto removes. As Solomon said in Proverbs 11:24, "One gives freely, yet grows all the richer; another withholds what he should give, and only suffers want."

God has placed people in my life who have given me life-giving words—words that affirm me, not belittle me. I have been told I am articulate and eloquent, which is so far from how I see myself, since I struggle to always convey my thoughts. I have received life-giving words about my mind. I have been told, "There is gold in there. You just need someone to mine it out." To have someone take the time to say that about my mind, which has always been a source of imprisonment for me, was gentle and freeing. My mind is truly a gift from God, and I never saw it that way. Now that I am focused on God's Word and God's truth, He reveals beautiful, uplifting, and joyful things worthy to be shared. My need for people, which felt like a weakness, is a means to draw out the gold that God has given me. As He revealed Himself to Moses, God, in His amazing patience and goodness, answered all my shortcomings with His presence and my fears with His worthiness. It does not matter who I am. It matters that God is with me and that He accepts me. It does not matter that I never know what to say to people because God, the mighty I AM, is enough.

My heart longs to yield everything to God, to stay in community with Him and to follow Him faithfully wherever He leads, but I have a tendency to veer off course, to seek favor, acceptance, and belonging outside of Him, even in good places like the community of the church. As I seek to be seen and accepted, rather than to accept and see, I find myself outside of God's promised rest. I feel isolated and alone. My heart makes comparisons to those around me. Jealousy courses through me, and I lose sight of who God created me to be. Shortly after I received the copies of my first published book, I felt compelled to offer them to the women of my Bible study. We had only been a group for a couple of months, but in a strange way, I felt like I fit in this Bible study more easily and more smoothly than any other Bible study that I had ever been a part of. The offering felt like the next step in the process of following God and His calling on my life to be bold in humility and love. What I discovered, however, was that when I made myself vulnerable, it exposed the same wound of not fitting in. Without consciously realizing it, in the offering, I looked for affirmation about whether I fit in. Somewhere in the process of trying to see people and welcome them, in those moments of vulnerability, I wanted to be seen and accepted. I hoped for feedback of some sort that being vulnerable in that way was meaningful to them somehow, but I heard nothing. Yet, within our study, another author, who is an engaging, bold, and lovely lady with a gripping, amazing story, offered one copy of her book, and it was flying around from reader to reader with much discussion of how amazing it was. These ladies were just being honest and real and not intentionally being hurtful, but it was so cutting to me. I did not maintain firm footing. I slipped. Where I was hoping to encourage the life of someone else, I found myself needing encouragement. I closed myself off from this group to protect myself. Every window to peek inside of me was boarded and shuttered up tight. I continued to attend our study, but I struggled to speak up. I no longer felt comfortable sharing from my heart and being vulnerable with my struggles. I felt rejected. I was no longer speaking up or communicating naturally. I disengaged from the group. I received the false impression that I did not belong and she did. The lie was that I was and always will be on the outside looking in. I bought into the lies the serpent hurled at me and isolated myself.

God intervenes in our lives by revealing Himself to us, as He did to Moses. He reveals that He is a holy fire who knows His people and intervenes for them but does not consume them. He is a God who comes. He revealed Himself to me through the story of Moses, showing me that He is a God who sends imperfect and unheard representatives, who find it difficult to speak up, on His own behalf and on behalf of His people, and that, when the time is right, people will hear the message we are sent with. God is a God who delivers. He is a God who leads us all our days and a God who teaches us to trust him. He chooses us and calls us so we must face our fears and so He can conquer them in His perfect love. We will conquer because

God remains with us. We will be victorious because God is I AM, and this name will be remembered through the generations.

Oh, the things God teaches Moses as they meet that speak into my life today! God not only shows Moses who He is as I AM, but God also reveals the authentic Moses to Moses. It is as if God is saying, "You are my fine, beautiful son delivered from the water, so you bring deliverance for My people. You are not out of place nor without a home. You have always belonged to me. I was equipping you in the house of Egypt. I am equipping you in the wilderness to become My servant. Your heart looked towards the plight of My people, and you intervened for them when you lived in the house of Pharaoh. You are a man I carefully crafted to rescue and protect. You were knit together as and have been prepared to be My appointed representative, prince, prophet, lawgiver, judge, and deliverer." God gives him multiple layers of affirmation. It taught Moses that he did, indeed, hear well from God, and it changed him. The Moses who led the people in the wilderness was not the same man who stood before God in these introductory chapters. Does it make you want to cry out, "God change me like you changed Moses"?

I completed that bio, and it consisted of my family, my occupation, where I live, and a few other personal details, but it did not contain nearly enough details about God's purposes and plans for my life. It did not encompass how He specifically knit me together. Ater reading these chapters in Exodus, I realize that the beauty of my transformation story was missing. As I consider a bio with God as the author of it, I see that the change from what I wrote would be dramatic:

"You are My deep well and My living waters flow through you. You do not have to speak loudly or often. Just be My well, and when people are thirsty, they will know where to come. I accept you even when you feel like no one else does. You have value and worth as My child. You do not have to toil and seek value and worth on your own. I have made you a visionary, able to see others, because you have always felt unseen. I want you to honestly share your struggles, telling others where their value and worth reside and about the freedom that this discovery brings. I have been equipping you to bring to me the person you really are and teaching you that transformation comes through asking. I will send you back to the source of your pain and your fear, but I will be with you in it, and you will be victorious. It does not matter that you struggle to

communicate, because I am not asking you to speak fancy words. I simply want you to share your heart, even the ugly, imperfect parts. You will share with the world that I desire honest hearts who seek Me over perfect ones and that transformation is something that I do for you, not something I expect from you."

I was sharing with a friend that I am currently feeling a bit overwhelmed by family, home, work, book writing, Bible study leadership, and blog posting, yet that God continues to show and reveal Himself to me in so many big and little ways. It is humbling and encourages me to regularly remain in a place of worship, praise, and rest. So, while I feel overwhelmed, I also feel blessed. She asked me, "In the moments that you feel overwhelmed, what do you do? Step back? Pray?" In the past the answer would have been to do more and continue to worry about it. I would scheme and come up with a plan of action. For so much of my life, I claimed Philippians 4:6–7 as my life verse. I was always seeking rest from my anxious moments. My mind was always going 100 miles per hour. I was not able to stop its force from driving fear, doubt, and anxiety into my body, knowing I needed to let God lead and handle my situation. But, while rationally knowing that, my brain was still constantly scheming to find a solution. I was crying out that I should lay my anxiety down but was not always able to lay it down. God finally connected the dots in my mind that the solution was in the very next verse. "Whatever is . . . think on those things." He has given me rest from my mental toiling by giving me an outlet for my mind. The desire to reach, touch, and impact the lives of other women has met me in my place of desperation and given me freedom. Whether or not books sell, blog posts are read, or podcasts are listened to, my mind focuses on what is just, lovely, pure, truthful, and commendable, and I am not held captive by my mind any longer. It is like the turning of a page in my life towards transformation. What I had envisioned as a way to help others has drastically helped me. My circumstances have not changed. The fear of the circumstances does not go away. What I choose to focus on is what has changed. Like the apostle Paul did, I "take captive every thought to make it obedient to Christ" (2 Corinthians 10:5b NIV).

The beautiful thing about writing freely, without an imminent deadline, is that it allows me to write when God lays something on my heart, and then I can set the book down when God is not encouraging me to write. It is in these quiet times that God is moving and positioning me to live out what I am writing about. I feel a passionate desire to write and get words on paper, and then I set it down without any burden to complete it. Some people thrive on deadlines and get their best work done within the deadline. God works differently through me. He's created me to ponder, write, live it out, ponder more as I'm living it out, and then write out what He's teaching me.

From a logical perspective, it seems crazy to have a book 90 percent complete and then let it sit for a year. But through everything that God is teaching me, He consistently reinforces that need for His timing. In that year of setting the book down, He was working so many other good things in my life all in line with His perfect timing. All the things I was praying through and asking for in chapter 1 were beginning to happen. So instead of just dreaming and writing about them, I was out there living them, walking through what God has set before me to walk through. While I waited on God to direct me on how to finish this book, God allowed me to write, disciple, mentor, and teach and made these things all part of what He has called me to do. I can hyperfocus on one thing so easily, but He is walking me through balance. So much of the time is spent making myself available to people and then waiting on God for the right moments and being focused on Him and others over myself. He has opened doors to so many amazing opportunities and moments that speak to my identity in Him and the value of making Him known. Let me give you a few examples:

1. The discipleship program that I was so anxious to be a part of was launched. It is a group geared towards pouring into working women and busy moms. God has brought all kinds of women, from all walks of life, beyond what we even anticipated. Most importantly, we are seeing women connect with one another, build community, and share the hard circumstances in their lives. God has granted me the privilege of being part of this leadership team and of teaching. Teaching was something my heart was drawn toward, but I never had the opportunity to do outside of kids' ministry. I've discovered that teaching God's Word is life-giving to me, not just intellectually teaching the Bible but teaching with authenticity—teaching in

a manner that conveys what God has taught me and what He has walked me through. I always walk away knowing that it was what I was born to do. God reveals His Word to me in special ways and entrusts me with sharing His Word with others. He delights me by allowing me to play a small part in meeting the needs of women and enriching their lives.

2. God has delighted me by showing me that I am a well like He revealed to me. He has brought family, friends, and coworkers to me when they need to talk. Sometimes I just listen, and I have nothing to offer but a heart of compassion and prayer. Sometimes, the Holy Spirit lays on my heart a question or a statement to share. When people are thirsty, they will come to the well just as God told me they would. I don't have to go searching for opportunities. I just need be available when God brings these divine appointments my way.
3. God has compelled me to venture into the scary and unknown, to meet people in their grief without an iota of understanding of what they are going through, and to be present with them despite my reservations and discomfort. I feel inept, but I want them to know that I see them, and I want them to see the love of Jesus in me. There is victory in not avoiding them in fear.
4. Since the summer of trying to connect and not connecting with women in my community, my heart has desired to pour into people in my community. God specifically laid a desire on my heart to get more involved in my children's band and drama programs at their school, through volunteering. God provides opportunities if we are willing. I was able to serve by organizing and serving dinners the week leading up to a show.
   Throughout the week I continually served with one mom. As the event drew near, circumstances transpired that publicly threw this mom's life into an upheaval, and she was hurting. God orchestrated a beautiful opportunity for me to be available and present, without being pushy, if she wanted to talk, and she did. I marvel at God's plan and His ability to patiently wait for me begrudgingly get on board and then to delight me by giving purpose to my offering. For so long, I have

avoided and groaned about putting myself out there and getting involved, and God seized the right time and plopped me in a situation to show grace and compassion when she needed it.

5. Sometimes He does more than we could even think to ask or imagine. God has impressed upon me a desire to share truth to the world through social media. I have founded a ministry aimed at helping people know what an abundant life in Jesus Christ looks like. Over the past year, with the community God has given me that was so difficult to come by, we have launched a podcast and ministry aimed at encouraging people, no matter where they are in their spiritual walk, to live fully in Christ's love.

Each of these moments were just that—moments of extraordinary work amid ordinary work that produced abundance in my life. These moments require patiently and faithfully showing up and being present for the opportunity to happen. When it does happen, because it will happen, celebrate the small wins that God uses as He moves to make big changes. These are moments that are not based on numbers. The abundance occurs in the opportunity to share truth. When and how God will use our small moments of victory is not what we should focus on. Our focus should be on the truth that *He will* use them, and He uses us to make those small moments possible. Praise God for His work. He impresses His good desires and plans on our hearts. He orchestrates the opportunities and moments for us to step toward what He has equipped us for, and He allows us to marvel that we are able to share in His life-giving transformative work in this way.

~

PAUSE TO PRAISE AND PONDER:

Theme: Living according to how God made us doesn't mean to give up everything we enjoy, but to use everything we enjoy for His glory.
Read Exodus 4:1–4.

Praise: How have you experienced God being with you? How have you known that you are upheld by God?

Brainstorming:

- What is (are) your biggest dream(s)?
- What is so appealing about your dream(s)?
- What is preventing you from attaining your dream(s)?
  - What are the biggest obstacles?
  - What are the biggest risks?
  - What is the sacrifice?
  - What is your biggest fear?

Get Creative:
- Draw a sandcastle on a shoreline with a bucket next to it. Write your bucket list items in the bucket. In the sandcastle, enter the ways your bucket list items could be used to further your own kingdom, which is built on shifting sand. In the bucket, enter the ways your bucket list items could be used for God's purposes.
- Draw a branch connected to a tree. Beside it, draw a staff that would be carved out of a branch. What are the differences between each branch?

- If God can use a dead piece of wood to display His power, imagine what He could do with a branch that abides in the vine. In what ways are you moving in your own power instead of abiding in the vine? How do you need to rest and be still?
- In what ways is your branch primed and ready to bear fruit? How is God calling you to move?

Daily Bread: In what ways can you bring God praise today? What is God personally calling you to? In what ways is He inviting you to rest and abide? In what ways is He inviting you to walk in the light?

- Draw a drinking glass. Select a verse related to what God has revealed to you today as you pondered that speaks truth about the ways and promises of God.

- Draw a sandwich
    - On the bottom bun, praise God by writing how you know that God created you uniquely for His specific purposes.
    - In the meat section of the sandwich, write one way that God is leading you. Consider the timing and write the destination (big dream or purpose) and then consider the next step in the journey that He is leading you to take.
    - On the top bun, write a truth contained in God's Word that speaks about resting and waiting on God and write a truth contained in God's Word that speaks about moving.

7

THE VAST WILDERNESS

Exodus 13:17-18, "*When Pharaoh let the people go, God did not lead them by way of the land of the Philistines, although that was near. For God said, 'Lest the people change their minds when they see war and return to Egypt.' But God led the people around by the way of the wilderness toward the Red Sea. And the people of Israel went up out of the land of Egypt equipped for battle.*"

My first taste of independence was not as joyous as I anticipated. I was all set to move into the dorms of college the weekend prior to the start of class for freshman orientation, only to receive the news that a beloved aunt had passed away, so instead of a fun new beginning with new friends and lasting memories, it was a quick dropping of my things into the dorm room, so we could go home to grieve and honor her life. I found myself at a funeral dealing with the emotions of losing someone special to me and processing my first real exposure to mourning the death of someone close to me. This death impacted my life. It was a hard and exhausting weekend. On Sunday, my brother dropped me off at school, and I wandered up through the hallway alone to begin this new stage of my life emotionally feeling every bit as alone as I physically was. I was extremely apprehensive. I entered my room still grieving and feeling like I missed out on my opportunity to meet people. I was sad and scared; I skipped lunch because I did not have the heart to go eat lunch by myself. And as I sat alone on my bed, numerous people came and left my room, in and out again, engaging with my roommate. They made plans together and all went off together to eat dinner, having the time of their lives. The entire time they flowed in and out, not one person spoke to me. In fact, not a single person even acknowledged me. I have never felt more invisible in my entire life. I was completely and utterly alone among a group. Finally, I knew I had to eat something, so I got up off my bed, feeling extremely sorry for myself, and moved towards the door, only to be leaving to go to dinner at the exact same time as my neighbor. She invited me to join her for dinner, and so began my college life. It took me years to recognize it because that is such a hurtful and vulnerable moment in my life, but, looking back, I can now see God's provision in that moment.

The Israelites experience their first taste of freedom as they venture out of Egypt towards the Promised Land. What an exciting time! All the milk and honey one could want. Surely, the pots of meat in Egypt will be nothing compared to the milk and honey God provides. What would you do with newly found freedom? What would your expectations be? With the mighty and powerful God on your side, it surely would be magnificent, everything you could imagine, especially with such a beautiful, victorious beginning. They start off strong and faithful, with a beautiful song of worship and praise. They give God the glory and honor He is worthy of (Exodus 15). There are joy and celebration, and then, all too quickly, the reality of life sets in. Soon enough, they find themselves without food and without water, questioning the wisdom of leaving the guarantee of sustenance behind even though that provision came at the cost of their freedom. The people are a mess. They all too quickly doubt and want to return to what they know, even knowing that it is not good for them.

God reveals to us why He does not immediately take the Israelites to the Promised Land. Exodus 13:17 tells us, "When Pharaoh let the people go, God did not lead them by way of the land of the Philistines, although that was near. For God said, 'Lest the people change their minds when they see war and return to Egypt.'" We often conclude that the Israelites were foolish and weak without considering our own natural bent to behave very similarly. What happens when you have gone through the blessed waters of deliverance, when you have seen God move and work in mighty ways, and all you experience are the waters of bitterness (Exodus 15:23), not the expected plentiful, abundant springs of water? What happens when you find yourself somewhere in between, no longer a slave but not really free? What happens when you are wandering with no place to belong, when you do not fit anywhere? You are no longer suffering and oppressed, but you are not joyful either. Dissatisfied, you feel bamboozled by the promise of deliverance that should lead to an abundance of sweet and satisfying things, but, when you look around, all you experience is want. *God, why did you rescue me only to let me die in the wilderness?* is a very real, genuine question to ask when our good God does not seem to be doing good things like meeting our basic needs or healing us. *Why are you allowing me to suffer?* God is not only concerned with delighting us. He is concerned with transforming us. God does not just deliver us from oppression and slavery. The meandering on His lit, roundabout path teaches us how to be *His* people. He is showing the Israelites how to serve Him and bring Him honor and glory once they are in the Promised Land.

We have come so far from the slavery of our past. We finally recognize our knowledge problem. God has revealed Himself to us. He called us by name out of the pit. He has invited us to come and see Him, to know Him by His words, His works, and His ways. This invitation is personal and humbling, and we trust Him to change our lives. Then, even with all this knowledge we've gained, sometimes we find ourselves wandering in the wilderness, seeing more removed from us than given to us and more taken than what we are willing to give up. The wilderness is a time of stripping away the temporal to focus on the eternal, a time of testing. It is a time of experiencing and coming to intimately know who God is. It shows us that when He calls us, it is not simply for our own enjoyment; it is for His purposes. As God promised the Israelites in Exodus 23:25, "You shall serve the LORD your God, and he will bless your bread and your water, and I will take sickness away from among you."

Nothing gives purpose and direction to our lives quite like the vast wilderness. Once again, we see God's paradox in action. What seems like relentless purposelessness, toil, and want is the preparation of God to enable us to bear fruit. What may seem like aimless wandering is the plan of God to teach His people purpose and direction. Romans 8:5–8 describes the reason for this teaching process: "For those who live according to the flesh set their minds on the things of the flesh, but those who live according to the Spirit set their minds on the things of the Spirit. For to set the mind on the flesh is death, but to set the mind on the Spirit is life and peace. For the mind that is set on the flesh is hostile to God, for it does not submit to God's law; indeed, it cannot. Those who are in the flesh cannot please God." God teaches His people so they will no longer live according to the flesh.

Though there is no greater joy than knowing God, walking in faith simultaneously produces, in one sense, and does not produce, in another sense, an immediate change of heart and mind. We are new creations, yet we need to learn to become more like Him. As Paul says in 2 Corinthians 5:17, "Therefore, if anyone is in Christ, he is a new creation. The old has passed away; behold, the new has come." God performs miracle after miracle in Egypt, claiming the people of Israel as His people while not requiring any action from them. He intentionally creates a division between the Israelites and the Egyptians and, in a few cases, spares the Israelites from the plagues inflicted upon the Egyptians. Exodus 8:22 gives one example, "But on that day I will set apart the land of Goshen, where my people dwell, so that no swarms of flies shall be there, that you may know that I am the LORD in the midst of the earth." On the verge of the tenth plague, however, we see God calling this group of people to go deeper, to begin actively following Him in faith. From that moment forward, God is teaching them to walk out their faith. When they go through the Red Sea, they walk out their faith by walking between walls of water. In the wilderness, they must trust God every day to provide for them. Day after day, they collect manna, just enough for that day. Day after day, they wait for the promise of the blessed land, not only learning whether they trust God but answering the most important question every follower of Jesus will face: "Even if I have nothing else, is having God as my God sufficient for me?" But, when the time finally comes for them to arise and go, they falter and do not lay claim to the promise, what they had been waiting for.

We know God through hearing about Him and then experiencing Him. We hear of Him through His Word and through the testimony of others. This is a unifying, universal, and global blessing that we, as believers, partake in together. Instead of harsh judgment against the actions of the

Israelites, if we strip away the amazing details of the book of Exodus and approach it from an overarching viewpoint, we see rebellion and a restoration story common to all whom God has called. As time moves on, people forget God and His ways. Entropy always occurs due to the wicked hearts of mankind. Favor and good things fade. People are forgotten. But God never forgets. He does not forget His promises, nor does he blot out our names in favor of the names of the more powerful. God knows His own by name and grants us favor even before we come to know Him. He makes His own fruitful and multiplies them. So, the world ruthlessly afflicts heavy burdens on us and schemes against us and ultimately against God. Yet, God's favor does not waver, and our favor is never defined by our circumstances. God deals well with, He sees, and He hears His beloved people in their struggles. Even in impossible situations, where we are at the end of what we can do, God delivers us in unlikely ways. He is the God of the impossible who shines forth as the God Most High, who orchestrates events and raises up people, calling them by name, at precisely the right time, to bring about deliverance and rescue.

There is defiance inside each of us, which leads to rage and rebellion. Violence reigns in our hearts, which results in more violence. Vengeance is our way. We look this way and that and sin when we think no one is watching, convinced that we hide our indiscretions. Even when we take matters into our own hands and make an irreversible, complete mess of our lives, God is working everything to the good of those who love him and are called according to his purpose (Romans 8:28). We run. We manage to find meager, unsatisfying rest, and a small measure of contentment, as we hide and heal. We avoid the calling and identity that God predetermined for us because we do not want to return to the pain of our pasts. We would rather be left alone, safe, and comfortable instead of being called and serving in uncomfortable situations. Where God longs to show us that the victory is in overcoming our past, we view the escape from our past as the victory. Not going back to where we fled from is our most pressing concern. We ignore the reality that people are suffering and need to be delivered, because our own fears and hurts drive our actions.

Then, the flame of God presents itself to us. The greatness of it draws us to Him. He calls us by name, and He reveals Himself to us. He makes Himself known, and then He makes us known, both to others and to ourselves, by revealing to us our purpose. He tells us that He is I AM who has chosen to send us, that He will grant us favor and victory even though the world will try to stop us. He will instruct us to lay down the lies. He walks us through the doubt toward our purpose and identity, and He puts in our hand the power and authority necessary to succeed, His sovereign power. The people He has called by name will believe, and He will rescue them through us. Our initial response is refusal. We dig in our heels, give voice to all our failings, and produce every excuse for God to send someone else. Yet, God always stays with us and does not give up on us. The One who knitted us together knows exactly what He created us for, and we cannot fail. Finally, begrudgingly, in obedience, we settle our affairs, and we follow.

God prepares the hearts of His people for the arrival of those He sends, and God gives us brothers and sisters to stand beside us in our mission. As God promises, people accept and believe. God's authority and His power are displayed to the world, yet the world refuses to submit to Him. Instead, unbelievers seek to display their own might by destroying God's people. Because of persecution, we question God, and then we question why God called us just to make things worse for others. God lovingly reminds us of His promises, and He reveals His purposes and His plans and asks us to trust Him.

When we share the words of God that have been entrusted to us with the hurting and enslaved, people's spirits are just too broken. They are too enslaved to sin to listen. But God always has plans to show people, not just tell people of, His deliverance. He makes the seed of faith grow. When favorable results do not instantaneously appear, we struggle to boldly speak of God's deliverance because we doubt God's abilities in our own lives. How can we speak with boldness and confidence when we ourselves doubt God? So, as we teach others about the goodness of God, God is simultaneously teaching *us* His goodness. We need to never forget whose house we belong to. We belong to the house of God. We have a legacy and heritage from Him. We are daughters and sons of the King, called for the purpose of speaking His name and His glory.

God converts our meager possessions and talents and mightily reveals His power. No offering is too small for God to use. At first, God may allow evil to mirror His authority, but evil cannot keep up with the majesty of our God. He reveals His superiority and leaves no one in doubt of who is truly mighty. Anyone who comes up against his plans will be swallowed up. The first plague points to God's supreme act of love and authority. Jesus's death on the cross turned flowing, living water to blood, and the resurrection restored Jesus back to flowing, living water, yet the world rejects His authority. So, God removes the plenty from the powerful. He usurps their power while displaying His authority over all creation. He requires them to acknowledge their sin and His superiority, even as they refuse to yield, resulting in their destruction and demise. God instructs us to remember His deliverance and gives us provision for the long journey ahead. God's wrath passes through the land of those who do not believe. Yet, He withholds His wrath for those who move in faith. The wrath of God is satisfied for those who are covered by the blood of the Lamb. God's justice and His merciful deliverance unite in one divine act. We come to know this God that is always working to deliver us from oppression and bondage. What is He working to deliver you from today?

We discover a newly found boldness and confidence as we are set free and as slavery is left behind. God does not take us along the paths we would choose, however, but along a carefully chosen path to teach us His ways and to teach us where we fear. We have seen His words fulfilled, His works displayed, and His deliverance, justice, and mercy made evident. Now, will we choose to follow Him in gratitude, or will we grumble and complain? Is He enough for us, or do our physical needs drive our satisfaction? He requires us to be consecrated, to serve Him only, and to follow where He leads. He remains with us through every step of our journey, a steady presence to look upon, trust, and follow. Our safety and security are constantly threatened, however. The enemy will not let us go without a fight. The enemy pursues us seeking our destruction. In terror, realizing that we are not mighty warriors, that we are nothing but freed slaves clothed in warrior garb, we watch the enemy approach. We are trapped. In these moments of terror, God places people in our lives to speak truth and wisdom. "Do not fear! Stand and watch God's rescue." God tests and requires that we act on our faith as He calls us to move forward and follow Him. Then God does the miraculous and brings us safely through. He devours our enemies, burying them forever; the waters of his wrath overtake them. Finally, terror comes upon the terrible. Once again, God's justice and his merciful deliverance unite in one divine act. We learn He is trustworthy and mightier than both our enemies and our fears as He destroys those targeting us. We discover that He is a God of war who fights our battles for us, instead of requiring us to fight His battles for Him. He is our power when we are overwhelmed and powerless. We can rest knowing that our God always fights for us.

When we follow God, He destroys our bondage and slavery. We witness His great power, we fear the Lord, and we believe. He becomes our own personal God, our God. We celebrate and sincerely worship with hearts full of gratitude and praise. But as we venture out on our journey led by God, not knowing where He is going, we experience want and need. Trials are brought before us to deepen our faith, our sincere praise dries up, and grumbling and complaining spew from our lips. God entreats us to trust Him and then shows us that we can trust Him. He teaches us His laws and His heart so we can please Him. When we are dissatisfied with our predicament, we seek others to blame and long for what was. Even though God has carried us safely through our bondage and slavery, we discover that our hearts have not fully relinquished our old worldly ways. As we go from plenty to want, from comfort to uncertainty, we flounder. We begin grumbling and quarreling. We look back with longing, forgetting the oppression and the bondage of the past. We long for what was, and we consider going back. God wants us to recognize and look toward His provision. God provides even as we grumble. He is teaching us to wait patiently with faith and to hunger and thirst for the right things. He heals in the bitter and hard things. He turns what is bitter to what is sweet. God provides daily, and what He provides is enough! Every day He asks for trust, obedience, and gratitude for the situations at hand. He asks for obedience instead of following what seems right in our own eyes. God promises His people not only deliverance but health, and we must be careful to diligently understand these promises of God. This is not a promise that focuses on the temporary nature of our lives here on earth. It is an everlasting deliverance and spiritual healing that goes beyond the prison walls and diseases found currently in our world. but we continuously focus on the temporal and on the threat of death. Yet faithfully, more faithfully than we deserve, God reveals more and more of Himself to us, revealing His glory, dwelling permanently with us.

Instead of trusting *and* waiting, we ungratefully demand God's miraculous favor in our lives. As we walk in His ways, enemies come and go, and God completely handles them. Yet He requires us to act, in a show of faith and obedience, not ever because He needs our help but to solidify our trust in Him. Acting as God wants us to act is exhausting and calls for us to patiently endure. Our enduring actions deeply affect the actions of those around us. God raises up helpers to support us when we are too weary to continue. We see victory and it teaches us to hold onto God's promises yet to be fulfilled. As we are tested and fail, God's mercy remains steady because our Rock is patient and kind. He was willingly stricken to provide living water, so we thirst no more.

God brings people into our lives to hear truth, to believe, and to speak truth to us in counsel. God teaches us to be a community of believers. We learn to take the time to share God's truth and to listen to wise counsel, to teach and delegate. God establishes us as His holy people and His treasured possession, a kingdom of priests and a holy nation. God gives us a beautiful glimpse of where He is leading us and asks the question, "Will you follow me?" God draws near and brings us to Himself at the foot of His holy mountain. We promise obedience and pledge ourselves to Him, but these things require consecration because God longs to dwell with us and His presence is a full sensory experience. It strikes fear and trembling into sinful man. But God is transforming us into His likeness. This jealous God who shows steadfast love to His people has requirements and rules for his people. The greatest of these rules is to love—first Him and then others. Because we are a special people to God, we are required to be different in both our heart and our actions. God requires a heart of sacrifice. He is a God who comes and a God who blesses those who follow His ways. As God continues to explain His laws, that explanation reveals His heart for love, restitution, and making everyone, no matter who, whole. It highlights mankind's bent toward selfishness, oppression, mistreatment, violence, grasping, lust, lies, and wickedness, and our need for someone to show us the way.

God shares His heart with us. God shares His plans with us. All things point to His glory and His saving sacrifice. He calls for us to willingly obey His commands, and He calls for us to be willingly generous. He consecrates us for His purposes. He has given us His Word, written with His finger, so that we can abide with Him and in Him. But during delay, when nothing seems to be happening and we no longer see God's mighty arm doing mighty things, we gleefully corrupt ourselves and begin to merrily worship idols, forgetting the God who rescued us from slavery. We latch onto inanimate objects and identify them as our means of rescue. Yet, no matter how we turn from Him, God relents from consuming us in His wrath. His promises of mercy and deliverance hold true. When faced with our sin, we distance ourselves from responsibility. We blame others for our choices. God ensures we recognize the weight of our sin, and that weight leads us to deeply mourn our actions.

As God accepts Moses's intercession for the people, graciously, God allows Jesus to make atonement for our sin and to intercede on our behalf. The one who does these things is one who understands that God being with us is what makes us special and distinct. God's favor rests on this man whose heart says, "If your presence will not go with me, do not bring us up from here," and that man experiences the glory of God and makes a way for us to experience God's glory as well. God responds with an acknowledgement of favor and allows his intercession on our behalf, because He knows His favored one by name. Now with a repentant heart, full of understanding that our reprieve is through the favor and the intercession of one man, we receive God's laws anew. We live with a gratitude that is expressed in unrestrained generosity that prepares the place to bring the extraordinary glory of God within the ordinary covering of man as He dwells within us. And in all things, all the words of the I AM are carried out and fulfilled.

Exodus is a beautiful story that is meant to work in our hearts to change us. It is meant to encourage us to long for a glimpse of God's glory. Whenever you read Exodus, I pray you do more than read it. I hope you engage in the story, that you join the Israelites in their trek across the vast wilderness, that you can put yourself in their place, experiencing the want and hardship in their pursuit of the land flowing with milk and honey, in their pursuit of the abundant life. As God conquered the Egyptian army, I imagine they thought that the hard times were behind them, and that this road was going to be easy, because they witnessed what God was capable of. If He were on their side, what could go wrong? When I imagine how they felt at the end of the book of Exodus on the cusp of the land of promise, my mind goes to *weary* or *worn*. Imagine how tired they were of the desolate wilderness; how ready they were for God's land of promise. But, instead of fully experiencing God and learning from Him, they test the Lord. They did not learn that God allowed them to wander and to go without, to teach them His sufficiency. Along the journey, their behavior worsens. They progress from grumbling and complaining to quarreling, to longing to stone Moses and Aaron, and ultimately to challenging Moses's authority, which was established by God. And when the time arrives, they do not go in. Fear holds them back. They refuse to enter His rest and instead of remembering His strong arm of deliverance, they long for Egypt once more to protect them. Paul's description of unbelievers in Philippians 3:19 could easily apply to the Israelites: "Their end is destruction, their god is their belly, and they glory in their shame, with minds set on earthly things." So, they find themselves worn and weary for thirty-eight more years. Do you feel worn today? Does life find you weary? Friend, what fear and old pattern of behavior is God calling to your mind to hand over to Him so you can enter His rest?

Have you ever stopped to consider the difference between Moses's experience with God and the Israelites' experience with God? Moses comes to know God, and he records what he learns in the first five books of the Bible, so future generations can come to know God as well. What moved Moses to ask for more of God, while the congregation seemed satisfied with less? In many ways, the Israelites appeared to be following Moses, not God. As soon as Moses disappears, they quickly turn to another god, as if they still had to come to know God themselves. We can learn the danger of following people, rather than following God, from them. They learned from Moses and recognized that I AM saved them, and they gave God honor and praise. There is acknowledgement of God's goodness and there is something unifying in the testimony of others, but to faithfully follow Him we must intimately know God ourselves. We cannot follow God by proxy through someone else. Thirteen times in Exodus God acts and credits His actions to making Himself known. Yet, it appears, while many often fear Him, their fear does not cause them to know Him.

We trust God and we trust His Word, but we tend to remain content latching onto the global truths and instructions contained within God's Word for all his people and forgo intimate moments of relationship with Him. We believe in these global truths, but they do not touch us in a personal way. Like the Israelites in the desert, we want deliverance, but we stand far off from the presence of God in fear. We may change some of the ways we behave, but it does not affect what we treasure because God is kept at a distance from our heart. When storms come attacking our real treasure, we grumble and complain, or we crumble in fear. As I take in the relationship between Moses and God, I see how transformational it was to Moses's life. It not only transformed his actions and how he loved the Israelites, it literally transformed his face. Exodus 34:34-35 describes this reality: "Whenever Moses went in before the LORD to speak with him, he would remove the veil, until he came out. And when he came out and told the people of Israel what he was commanded, the people of Israel would see the face of Moses, that the skin of Moses' face was shining. And Moses would put the veil over his face again, until he went in to speak with him." When I take in the Israelites and their intermittent faithfulness, I cannot help but question the difference. Why was he so transformed while others remained so shakable? *Lord, how do I become so transformed that I stay wholly and completely focused on you, so that anyone who looks at me sees the difference in me because it has transformed my face?*

A friend of mine who is extremely relational shared her difficulties with diligently, consistently spending time with God: "I know He is here. I know He is with me, but it is not like I can see Him sitting across from me. It is just different, so it is hard." For years this was my experience too—knowing that He is with me, knowing He loves me, but not experiencing the promised fullness of His presence and the overwhelming, life-altering joy of knowing Him. I was left thinking, *Is this all there is to this spiritual walk?* If I am truly honest, I was underwhelmed. I knew about His goodness. I sober-mindedly tried to remain self-controlled to do what I should do and not do what I should not do. But God's invitation is first to come and see and then to follow Him. How do you hear from God? How are you witnessing His ways today? Slow down and give God space and time to move in your mind and then in your heart. Stop seeking advice solely from books and other people and begin taking your concerns to God and wait for Him to answer. Enjoy the process of conversing with our Creator God. Read His Word and listen. I stopped focusing on trying to do what I knew I should do and just began asking God to help me know Him more. The more I came to know Him—His goodness and grace—the more my heart longed to be like Him, the more the call to obedience became something I wanted to do, not something I shamefully avoided or half-heartedly attempted.

During their time in the wilderness, the Israelites discovered that slavery masks itself enticingly in plenty. When we only focus on our physical well-being, we remain slaves forever. Exodus 16:3 (NIV) expresses their attitude: "The Israelites said to them, 'If only we had died by the LORD's hand in Egypt! There we sat around pots of meat and ate all the food we wanted, but you have brought us out into this desert to starve this entire assembly to death.'" They reduced their identity to their bellies. For this doubtful bunch, the path to abundance looked very much like certain death, and the path to death looked enticingly like abundance. To people uncertain of where they would find both food and water, a barren wasteland hardly evokes confidence of abundance. But God's inscrutable, brilliant ways rarely make sense to us. Usually, gaining abundance first means you must let go of the meager to take hold of the extraordinary and the plentiful, though the extraordinary and the plentiful are not yet in sight. What does it feel like to totally and completely rest on promises that you cannot see? What does it feel like to completely let go and have nothing whatsoever grasped in your hands? It feels like authentic, working, and moving faith. 1 Peter 1:7-8 speaks of this faith and its results: "so that the tested genuineness of your faith—more precious than gold that perishes though it is tested by fire—may be found to result in praise and glory and honor at the revelation of Jesus Christ."

Like He did at the Garden of Eden and the Tower of Babel, God intervenes to prevent catastrophic results to lead us towards a greater consecrated purpose. If we look at both interventions, we see a cutting off, a thwarting that stings as it happens and leaves us questioning God's goodness. In Eden, man is removed from paradise, the only home we ever knew, and sent out to tend the cursed ground for ourselves, yet God was preventing us from permanently staying in our death state. He was protecting us from ourselves. This banishment led us toward rescue. At Babel, what seems like separation and the birth of disunity is actually God confusing and separating evil intent so it loses its momentum and power. His acts that seem like cutting off and ripping away are acts of His grace and mercy to bring us deliverance.

In reference to our purpose, I hear phrases like, "We are to know him and to make Him known," and I consider the perspective of that statement. While I do not disagree, is our view still a bit distorted? Making Him known, by professing Him, does not necessarily mean that you allow yourself to be known and exposed by Him. We can continue to hide parts of ourselves in darkness and sin and, like hypocrites, still live and speak of the goodness of God. Could the lens of the microscope be dialed in a little bit more for a crisper view? Does it clarify things when we recognize that it is not us at all, but rather God, who makes Himself known? God makes Himself known, and His works are established for us to walk in. What right do we have to boast or claim anything? As Paul asked the Corinthians in 1 Corinthians 4:7b, "What do you have that you did not receive? If then you received it, why do you boast as if you did not receive it?" While we have a responsibility to move differently based on the grace we have received, we cannot hold our efforts and our desire to know Him pridefully because it is God who has revealed Himself to us, it is Jesus who has reconciled us to the Father, and it is God who is refining us. God leads our way, intentionally walking us through things because He knows us. We are in a similar situation to the Israelites, of whom it is said in Exodus 13:17, "When Pharaoh let the people go, God did not lead them by way of the land of the Philistines, although that was near. For God said, 'Lest the people change their minds when they see war and return to Egypt.'" God's grace prevents us from turning back and going where He is not leading. Maybe our focus should center on being known, on revealing everything to Him, and on not hiding or withholding anything from Him. To be known means that we make Him known—there is no other response. It is a natural outpouring because at the end of being known is a comprehension of grace alone, that there is nothing within us to boast of or that draws God's favor towards us. I consider Moses, and I think of how God refers to him as the one with whom he speaks with face to face, with no barriers between them. We find this description in Numbers 12:6-8: "And he said, 'Hear my words: If there is a prophet among you, I the LORD make myself known to him in a vision; I speak with him in a dream. Not so with my servant Moses. He is faithful in all my house. With him I speak mouth to mouth, clearly, and not in riddles, and he beholds the form of the LORD. Why then were you not afraid to speak against my servant Moses?'" *Lord God, reveal to me my sin so there are no barriers between us, so I can know you intimately and fully.*

During my Lenten journey that I referred to earlier, I asked God to show me what I was clutching tightly to that I needed to let go of. Immediately after asking, I sensed God prompting me to step down from an area of service in my church. Seeking to affirm that I heard correctly, I asked God why I would step down without having something to take its place, and I sensed that God wanted me to be ready for something. It was hard, not only because God called me to this ministry eight years earlier but also because I love to serve. I want to volunteer at my church. With difficulty I stepped down. I had nothing concrete to take its place, so I feared that people would think I was unwilling to serve, not that I was walking in obedience. It was a venture of faith to trust God with my reputation. As I waited for what I was to be ready for, I prayed. I sought God through His Word. I searched my heart and continued to pray, waiting for God's guidance about what I was to be ready for.

I did not have an automatic understanding of what God was leading me to. Some people seem to just know what they were born to do. That has not been my experience. My life has been a struggle for self-identity. I have never understood where I fit in. I do not have a strong sense of what I was made for. I was not able to stand on knowing who God made me to be because I did not have a sense of who God made me to be. I furiously worked to be the best at everything to validate my worth, so competition and jealousy easily run rampant in my heart, even though I try to hide them. Invariably, these negative qualities ooze and creep out. That is what sin does. It seeps out of us no matter how hard we try to keep it in. Let me give an illustration. A friend of my college friend came to visit on campus. The three of us sat down together to play a trivia game. On the floor of our dorm, I was known to be one of the better trivia players. It was a way for me to stand out, so it provided a sense of identity for me. As we played, she soundly beat me. She crushed me, but not only at trivia; she demolished my sense of value and worth by removing my identity of being special at something within the hallway of the dorm. What happens when someone comes along who is better than you are at what makes you special? It is demoralizing. It becomes about so much more than a silly game. She was playing a game, but it was destroying something real in me—the value and identity that I had given myself. I tried to be good-natured about it all, but the more she handily beat me, the more unable I was to hide how upset it made me, how it personally affected me.

Twenty years after that day, I still struggle to know what I am made for, to rest in who I am and not make comparisons with others. As I prayed, discipleship, especially talking to people about an abundant life, was continually and overwhelmingly on my heart. I long to share, but my natural demeanor is not conducive to meeting new people and having conversations with them. I get so frustrated with myself and how I avoid people because I am not able to easily and comfortably engage in conversation. I question what I can possibly do for God's kingdom when I so often prefer to be alone. How do I overcome all the social anxieties I possess? Really, being known is scary for me because it could result in rejection or ridicule. It allows people to see the veneer a little more closely—that there are cracks in it, not polished perfection.

So, as I waited and prayed for what I needed to be ready for, puzzle pieces came into focus bit by bit. It began with bits of understanding regarding the change that comes into our lives when we have a proper, balanced view of God in comparison to ourselves. God is justice and mercy, power and love. He is the King worthy of honor, obedience, and praise, but He humbles Himself to draw near to us, to enter the pit to draw us out, and to call us His friends. How necessary it is for us to see and understand what mankind, in his heart, is capable of without God and what God transforms the hearts of people into when they are set apart and known by Him. The view of all these pieces, properly seen in light of one another, creates a gratitude and a longing to serve, a desire to please the Lord, not because we are seeking a righteousness that we could never earn to receive His favor but because we have His unmerited favor and we long to be more like Him.

I stored up in my heart each thing revealed, until the whole took shape into something that I could share with others. As I wondered and pondered, I journaled, wrote, reflected, and pursued Him, and He never ceased to meet me and commune with me. He revealed to me His good purposes and His heart. As I consider His use of sharing small pieces of a puzzle with me instead of just plainly speaking to me in phrases, I realize that this is a playful way that He engages me and speaks to me uniquely. You see, I am a ponderer and a problem solver. I love puzzles, so He engages me, His own, whom He intimately knows and whom He created to problem solve, by giving me little pieces of a puzzle at a time to put things together. It is not that He does not or cannot speak to me in other ways, but there is something so sweet about knowing that He chooses to speak with me, through His Word, in a manner that is unique to how He created me, because He knows me.

I get bits and pieces, and I know in my heart that there is a link, that God is revealing something to me. I know He is leading me down a path and I just have to be patient for the pieces to fall into place. It is both exciting and humbling. It keeps me from getting prideful, and it also drives the desire in my heart to know God more and to stay in community with Him. I have heard so many times that it is better to keep things simple and not to overcomplicate things. It can be so piercing for me to hear those words, because it leaves me feeling that how I am naturally wired is not right, that it is dangerous for people, somehow. There is something inherent in me that struggles with simplicity, because I do not know what to do with it. I naturally take something simple, and I consider it. I ponder it. I look at its opposite, I consider words or things like it, and I question how my heart receives it. I consider how God has shown me the truth of that phrase in my past experiences, or how He might be showing me the truth of that phrase in my current life situations. To so many, this probably seems exhausting, but, to me, these conversations, puzzle-piece-receiving revelations, and eventual deeper understanding of who God is and how His Word interrelates are exhilarating to me. It is life-giving, and I look forward to this time with God. He has wired within me a natural love for and inclination to meditate on His Law, day and night, and a desire to know Him more by taking the time to ponder His ways. I absolutely cherish God's Word and His ways. God is a God who puts the puzzle pieces into place.

Long before the words of this book were written, I envisioned the front cover image of this book. I could see the vibrant puzzle pieces on a white background, the puzzle mostly complete, displaying identity images while spelling out the word *Known*. The title speaks of the importance of knowing and being known to make known. As we come to know and understand the truth of who we are in Him, the more we move in obedience to make Him known. The white background represents the transformative radiance and purity that He brings to our lives, the vibrant colors represent the vibrant life of abundance He provides, and the images represent the worth, purpose, and identity that He brings to our lives. They both reflect the church's identity in Christ and represent who I am, specifically and personally, in God. The images are made up of puzzle pieces because that reflects how God reveals His truth to me, piece by piece, each beautiful and unique on their own, but when put together revealing a fuller, grander picture of Him, His love, and His story. The puzzle is not fully put together because we are still learning and growing and not yet brought to completion.

I laugh at the irony of the puzzle piece imagery because, in many ways, I am a puzzle to myself. It took me a long time to realize that I needed God to put the puzzle pieces of me into place. I am not someone who naturally knows or understands who I am and what I am made for. I have always felt too different, too complicated, and too serious for the world around me. I did not understand why I would not speak up when I wanted to be seen, why things would make me angry or defensive, or why all negative comments would cause me to spiral uncontrollably. I was a jumbled mess that did not know who I was or how I fit, so any criticism demolished my worth. God had to fit each piece into place, patiently revealing me to me, to show me the picture of how He sees me and how I needed to relinquish how I see me. He calms me. He orders and organizes my internal chaos for a purpose.

I first began asking God what my unique identity in Him was while I was waiting for Him to reveal to me what I needed to be ready for. As I prayed, the first word I heard was *authentic*. For much of my life, I have hidden myself out of fear of rejection. Being led through the vast wilderness has shown me that God is enough for me. My identity, value, and worth are determined by Him alone, so all those hidden things—the fears, the things that make me different, the over-thinking—are all to be used for God's purposes and for His glory. As I continued to seek Him and to understand how to move in service and obedience to Him, He revealed to me that I am His problem solver and His innovator. I realized that my critiquing is not all bad. It can be and is a good thing. For so long, I viewed it only as an indication of my inability to be satisfied. Innovation is the recognition that the current state is not ideal, that it can be improved. It is the ability to assess and analyze and determine what is the cause of the problem and to obtain an understanding of what should be enhanced. It is this characteristic within me that keeps me asking, *God, do not allow me to be satisfied with my current level of what I willingly give You. Keep showing me my heart and the ways I am complacent, manipulative, disdainful, unloving toward others, and often angry and bitter. Enhance me. Bring me more and more into Your likeness.* This tendency toward critiquing is what keeps me praying for others to authentically know and serve our great Creator.

I am thankful and grateful to God for showing me how I am uniquely made, for enabling me to let go of the impulse to compare myself to others and the need to be perfect, but I still have difficulty understanding how I am effective in the Kingdom of God. The truth is that I am not a talker. I am very reserved. I never know what to say, and I do not have the ability to think of what to say quickly. I need time to process and ponder my words. I never want to speak without thinking. All too often, I, like a coward, avoid putting myself in these positions. These personal attributes seem counter-productive to spreading the good news and teaching God's Word. As I continued to pray and seek opportunities to reach others and encourage others in truth, God showed me that I am His well, that He brings those who are thirsty to the well, and that arising and going does not have to include being a social butterfly but can simply involve having my eyes open and being available when the thirsty come to the well.

What are your greatest hardships and how is God looking to restore them? How has God uniquely made you? I never dreamed that God would call me to write. I chose a career that had a linear, formulaic bent, something that I easily understood, something I was good at, so I was guaranteed to have the "right" answer. Nothing was abstract or creative. Sometimes I think, "How could you know yourself so little and have so little confidence in yourself? No wonder nobody else knows you. You could not even see yourself." What is amazing is that God leads us to our purposes in Him. He addresses all our fears as He addressed all of Moses's fears. They were conquered and irrelevant the moment Moses came to know the living God, but God had to first relieve him of the poison and the lies he harbored inside.

~

PAUSE TO PRAISE AND PONDER:

Theme: God leads us on a journey to teach us how to be citizens in His Kingdom.
Read Exodus 13:17–18.

Praise: How have you experienced the presence of God in the worst times in your life? How have you experienced God in the best times of your life?

Brainstorming:

- What are your three biggest wants in life?
- What are your three biggest needs in life?
- Reflect on the worst times in your life. How has God brought good from them?
- Consider a time that you longed for freedom from something, and when you were freed from it, you felt underwhelmed by that freedom? How have you looked back and wanted to be under its rule again?

Get Creative:
- Take your three biggest wants and your three biggest needs and write them in the blank of the following sentence, "Even if you don't ___________________________, Jesus, you are enough for me."
- Draw a mosaic. Within the pieces, write the various parts of yourself. Include strengths and weaknesses. Do your best to fill as many pieces as you can. Then color the pieces, representing how God makes beauty from our brokenness.
- Draw a second mosaic. Consider how the body of Christ is also broken pieces fitted together into a mosaic. This time, only color in one piece, representing you. Ask God how you should work within the body of Christ.

Daily Bread: In what ways can you bring God praise today? What is God teaching you about Himself? How is God calling you to be a part of the body of Christ?

- Draw a drinking glass. Select a verse related to what God has revealed to you today as you pondered that speaks truth about the ways and promises of God.
- Draw a sandwich.
    - On the bottom bun, praise God by writing how you know that God created you to be a vital part of the body of Christ.
    - In the meat section of the sandwich, write one way that you feel broken that God is using to create a mosaic. How is God leading you to be a part of the body of Christ?
    - On the top bun, write a truth contained in God's Word that speaks about the body of Christ and our need for one another and a verse that speaks about the trials of life.

8

THE GLORIOUS TABERNACLE

Exodus 40:34 *Then the cloud covered the tent of meeting, and the glory of the* L*ORD filled the tabernacle.*

One of my favorite aspects of my home is the property it sits upon. With the luxury of ten acres tucked away from bustling city life, my favorite activity is listening to the sound of the wind rustling through the towering trees. We have maples, oaks, elms, walnuts, apple trees, and mulberry trees. I am surrounded on every side by this beautiful artistry and symphony of God's creation. On our property is an entire grove of apple trees. These trees were cared for and pruned by my husband's grandfather but left unattended after his death. For years, these trees were left to grow wild and unruly, and they have grown so tall that harvesting the apples is now impossible. The apples fall uselessly to the ground to rot. This rotting fruit littering the ground is not only worthless, but it also becomes a liability. What was meant to be consumed and to provide sweet nutrients has become a slick, stinky ankle-turning and slipping hazard.

In the exodus from Egypt, God displayed His might. God delivered them and made Himself known. The people of Israel saw Him, and they knew that He alone was the LORD their God. If the purpose of our Christian walk was deliverance alone, the book of Exodus could have stopped at chapter 14 as soon as the Israelites crossed the Red Sea. Instead, we learn of God intentionally leading the Israelites the long way around so they could endure hardships to learn to rely on God, while also discovering God's glorious presence in their midst. Thankfully, God, the vinedresser, does not leave our hearts unattended to fall uselessly to the ground, rot, and become a liability. He prunes us to be useful for His good purposes. In the middle of the wilderness, somewhere between the deliverance from oppression and rest in God's Promised Land, God constructs His tabernacle, and it is glorious. Acting in obedience and diligence, the people of Israel specifically carry out God's detailed design. They use their time, resources, and talents, working together for the common goal of accomplishing God's will.

The focus of the Bible is predominantly on disobedience and hardship. Imagine with me all the periods of plenty and goodness that are not recorded in the Bible compared to the amount of hardship and disobedience that is recorded. Why? Because it highlights not only that we quickly and easily fall away but also that He is the God in the hard and the God who gives grace to the disobedient. *Lord, let me not focus on the waters that are about to sweep over my head, but on You, who keeps them at bay. Let me focus on You, my Good Shepherd, knowing You are leading me to green pastures and still waters, even when my eyes and my mind want to believe my surroundings seal my fate.* We should see that God has so much more in store for His people than a land of promise in wickedness, without leadership or wisdom. He patiently molds us so we can know Him intimately, so we trust Him with everything that we hold dear, and so we are obedient and willingly allow ourselves to be used for His purposes. All too often, we want the deliverance but do not want the challenge of following Him faithfully. We want spiritual maturity, but we do not want to traverse the vast desert to receive it. We always want an abundance of food and water, and we want it now.

In the lack and the wandering, the Israelites consistently looked back towards Egypt with longing. When we are in the same situation, God Himself appears to us in our confusion and misery, shining forth while we are still focused on the world (John 1:11). God draws near and invites us to come and see! This is precisely what Jesus did with His first disciples in John 1:38-39a: "Jesus turned and saw them following and said to them, 'What are you seeking?' and they said to him, 'Rabbi' (which means

Teacher), 'Where are you staying?' He said to them, 'Come and you will see.'" God desires to see us stop running from Him and to see us turn back towards Him. He desires to rescue us from our terrible, binding choices of ugliness and sin. His desire is that we all turn from our ways to trust in His Son, Jesus, God's perfect sacrifice. The apostles made their recognition of this clear in Acts 4:12, when they said, "And there is salvation in on one else, for there is no other name under heaven given among men by which we must be saved."

God calls Bezalel, meaning "in the shadow of God," and Oholiab, meaning "Father's tent," by name to craft the items in the tabernacle. God's Spirit gives them the knowledge and the skill to complete the task (Exodus 31:1–8). But do not miss that, while only two are named in Scripture, every single person who contributes to the construction of the tabernacle is called by name for such a purpose. The Israelites continually brought freewill offerings to Moses in such abundance that the craftsmen approached Moses about it, saying, "The people bring much more than enough for doing the work that the LORD has commanded us to do." And Moses restrained the people from bringing any more contributions (Exodus 36:3–7 ESV). With all the grumbling, complaining, and talk of returning to Egypt, why the sudden change of heart? How do they move from stiltedly obeying to such all-in, unrestrained generosity? To understand the change, we must look at what occurred in their lives just prior to the tabernacle's construction.

As God was giving Moses the instructions for the tabernacle, the people of Israel were committing a great sin. Even when we recognize God's deliverance and follow Him, situations tend to draw us back towards our old lives. There is a pull in us towards slavery. The Israelites followed Moses until he disappeared for a time. During the wait, their hearts turned towards other gods. Exodus 32:1-4 describes their change of heart and what they did because of it: "When the people saw that Moses delayed to come down from the mountain, the people gathered themselves together to Aaron and said to him, 'Up, make us gods who shall go before us. As for this Moses, the man who brought us up out of the land of Egypt, we do not know what has become of him.' So Aaron said to them, 'Take off the rings of gold that are in the ears of your wives, your sons, and your daughters, and bring them to me.' So all the people took off the rings of gold that were in their ears and brought them to Aaron. And he received the gold from their hand and fashioned it with a graving tool and made a golden calf. And they said, 'These are your gods, O Israel, who brought you up out of the land of Egypt!'" The presentation of the laws, the tabernacle, and the order and ordaining of the priests in the later chapters of Exodus shows us God's intent for His people. Yet, as God is laying out His ways, His people turn from Him. The golden calf clearly shows us the difference between our bent and God's intent for us. God's plans are to make us holy and set apart, and we are stiff-necked and struggle to turn away from our sin. In our walk, we recognize His deliverance, and we follow. Yet difficult situations and uncertainty draw us back toward our old lives.

Understandably, God's anger burned against their corrupt hearts and against their rejection of His leadership. On behalf of the people, Moses approached God to make atonement for them. He pleaded with God to spare them. God's punishment of removing Himself and sending an angel to lead the people was just and fitting for their sin of denying His leadership. God declares this punishment in Exodus 33:3, "Go up to a land flowing with milk and honey; but I will not go up among you, lest I consume you on the way, for you are a stiff-necked people."

For the first time, these people recognize the weight of their actions, they authentically mourn their sin, and, for one glorious moment, everything was held by the people of Israel in proper balance. They recognized the proper view of the righteousness of our God who draws near to us, their undeserving unrighteous, and they were grateful. What a privilege and an honor to have God in their midst, and they were at risk of losing it due to their disregard of Him and what He had done for them! God's mercy is always on display, even in His anger. He beautifully restores these people as He and Moses converse. Exodus 33:13–14 gives us part of their discussion: "'Now therefore, if I have found favor in your sight, please show me your ways, that I may know you in order to find favor in your sight. Consider too that this nation is your people.' And he said, 'My presence with go with you, and I will give you rest.'" We participate in one form of debauchery after another. God's wrath is just towards our actions and our wayward hearts, yet, just as we witness God extending grace to the people of Israel due to Moses, God withholds His wrath and extends mercy and compassion to us through the favor of Jesus.

God keeps His promises not based on Israel's faithfulness but on God's own grace and mercy.

Their newly found gratitude came from this understanding of God's abounding mercy. God does not abandon them, when He justly could have consumed them in His anger. God chooses, instead, to extend grace despite their faithlessness, and this understanding has the greatest impact on their wayward hearts. This knowledge stirs action and a desire to respond to God with faithfulness and love because of the generosity of God's steadfast love that is bestowed upon them. Humility generates gratitude. Gratitude generates generosity, and, for a time, they became unrestrained in their generosity. And in the middle of the hard things, when our hearts are full of gratitude towards God for remaining faithfully with the unfaithful, the extraordinary is born amid the ordinary. A consecrated place for the glory of God to dwell is established.

The intricacies of the design and the value of the materials donated are not what makes the tabernacle so glorious, although, with the amazing carved details, with the bronze, silver, and gold, I am sure it was a sight to behold. This amazing, moving, and communal place to meet and worship was glorious because God chose to dwell among these people, and this tent was the place where the glory of God dwelled. John echoes this image when he describes Jesus coming to earth in John 1:14, "And the Word became flesh and dwelt among us, and we have seen his glory, glory as of the only Son from the Father, full of grace and truth." The Israelites plundered the Egyptians when they exited Egypt, receiving presents from God to one day be used for the gift of the presence of God. By giving, they all enjoyed and benefited from the presence of God. To *restrain* is to "restrict, withhold, keep back, or forbid." Can we dare to ask, *Lord, help me to have a spirit so generous that I need to be restrained from bringing more*?

The presence of God, in our midst, is a full sensory experience that changes the space that it inhabits into something extraordinary. Exodus 19:16 describes such an experience: "On the morning of the third day there were thunders and lightnings and a thick cloud on the mountain and a very loud trumpet blast, so that all the people in the camp trembled." They saw His presence. They heard His presence. They felt His presence. And they quaked in fear because our unholy flesh would perish in His holy presence. What belongs to God is to be sanctified, set apart, and holy to serve Him.

Exodus 19:10 says, "The Lord said to Moses, 'Go to the people and consecrate them today and tomorrow and let them wash their garments.'" It was not an immediate, casual interaction. It was something that took days to prepare for. For three days the people prepared themselves for the presence of the Lord.

God was very detailed with each piece of His tabernacle. The curtains were made of fine twined linen of blue, purple and scarlet; cherubim were woven into the fabric. God's mercy seat was made of gold and had hammered cherubim across its top. Hammered almond blossoms were created on the lampstand. God's plans for His dwelling place were intricate and filled with imagery and beauty. Just as it took time for Bezalel and Oholiab to carefully and meticulously craft each item in the tabernacle, God carefully and meticulously crafts us, His tabernacle, for His glorious, holy presence. God is not just simply with us. He is *in* us. We are the tabernacle in which God chose to allow His glory to dwell. Do you see the nature of God's dwelling place and what it means for us? He dwells in us so we can dwell in the shadow of Him. Once again, we see God's intricate, detailed plan in action to the most minute detail. He uses even the meaning of His craftsmen's names to reveal His perfect plan and precision. The "Father's tent" provides us the ability to dwell "in the shadow of God."

In 1 Corinthians 3:16, Paul carries this language into the New Testament: "Do you not know that you are God's temple and that God's Spirit dwells in you?" This moving dwelling place of God represents us, His church, those who have come and seen His goodness, those who have chosen to follow Him. 2 Corinthians 5:1–5 applies this language to our physical bodies: "For we know that if the tent (tabernacle) that is our earthly home is destroyed, we have a building from God, a house not made with hands, eternal in the heavens. For in this tent we groan, longing to put on our heavenly dwelling, if indeed by putting it on we may not be found naked. For while we are still in this tent, we groan, being burdened—not that we would be unclothed, but that we would be further clothed, so that what is mortal may be swallowed up by life. He who has prepared us for this very thing is God, who has given us the Spirit as a guarantee." When we know God and are known by God, He reveals to us that He not only dwells within our midst but that He dwells within us. His plan is to consecrate us, His tabernacle, and to make us holy. Peter reveals this in 1 Peter 1:15-16:

"but as he who called you is holy, you also be holy in all your conduct, since it is written, 'You shall be holy, for I am holy.'" Like the tabernacle of old, our bodies are the ordinary covering over the extraordinary place where God dwells.

Exodus 40:34–38 says, "Then the cloud covered the tent of meeting, and the glory of the LORD filled the tabernacle. And Moses was not able to enter the tent of meeting because the cloud settled on it, and the glory of the LORD filled the tabernacle. Throughout all their journeys, whenever the cloud was taken up from over the tabernacle, the people of Israel would set out. But if the cloud was not taken up, then they did not set out till the day that it was taken up. For the cloud of the LORD was on the tabernacle by day, and fire was in it by night, in the sight of all the house of Israel throughout all their journeys." We are the moving tabernacle, the tent which houses the glory of God. We are the moving testimony of His faithfulness, His deliverance, and His guidance. As He moves, we are to move. Arising and going is as natural to our calling as following Him, because He is a sending God. As God first sent Moses and then sent His Son to deliver His people, God sends all His people to make disciples of all nations (Matthew 28:18–20). God's redemption leads to service. Leviticus 20:26 (NIV) says, "You are to be holy to me because I, the LORD, am holy, and I have set you apart from the nations to be my own." Following Him includes arising and going and being holy.

Exodus ends with the erection of the tabernacle and the presence of God among the people guiding them, not with the entrance into the Promised Land as one would expect. The book stops while they are in the middle of their journey. What an amazing observation to contemplate! If the journey is to arrive at the Promised Land, why does Moses stop the book of Exodus at this moment? This destination was special and promised by God, but no destination will ever compare to the presence of our holy, loving God dwelling in our midst. The book ends by highlighting the truth of God's words to Moses. Exodus 34:6–7 says, "The LORD passed before him and proclaimed, 'The LORD, the LORD, a God me thirty-eightrciful and gracious, slow to anger, and abounding in steadfast love and faithfulness, keeping steadfast love for thousands, forgiving iniquity and transgression and sin, but who will by no means clear the guilty, visiting the iniquity of the fathers on the children and the children's children, to the third and fourth generation.'"

Now that the glory of God is among them, do they follow Yahweh all their days? The end offers hope that they will follow and intimately know this unparalleled God of mercy and grace dwelling among them, that they will courageously and boldly follow Him in obedience, without revealing whether they do. It evokes a question in our hearts, "What will I do? Will I follow and intimately know this unparalleled God of mercy and grace dwelling in me?" In the book of Numbers, we discover that they do not enter the Promised Land for thirty-eight more years. Yet, God's presence steadfastly remains with them. Despite the consequence of many more years in the wilderness, God's mercies are new every morning as He remains with them day after day.

We then see a picture of a proper response to God through Moses. His interaction with God is so beautiful. It is not about the Promised Land. It is about God making us distinct and set apart. It is a knowledge that runs deep that I am so secure in His goodness and that He knows me so well that I rest with the knowledge that everything that I endure has a purpose. I do not say that flippantly, with the phrase that solves all things, "You just have to have faith!", as if to sweep my concerns and struggles away with an empowering anthem. I say that with a raw and bleeding heart, desiring that God removes what is causing me anguish, but even if He does not, I trust Him. My clinging to Him and my praise of Him is not and should never be based on my present situation. It has been established on the very nature and character of God. As misguided as the Egyptians were for challenging the might of God, the Israelites were also misguided in doubting Him. How easily we see misguidance in others, but, at the same time, how often we cannot see it within ourselves! Their choices do not need to be our choices. Their delay and doubt do not indicate that we will delay and doubt. Yet, even if I find myself challenging God's authority or doubting His abilities, God continuously protects me and provides me shelter despite my frailty.

How will you respond? Will you respond as a loyal and trusted friend, with your heart aligned with Him, with gratitude, unrestrained generosity, and living out your days in courage and faith, or will you long for what was and desire and encourage others to turn back, like the dog or the pig who tramples the treasures of heaven underfoot? Do you find yourself tired of waiting on God? Do not be like the Israelites described in Numbers 14:2–4, "And all the people of Israel grumbled against Moses and Aaron. The whole congregation said to them, 'Would that we had died in the land of Egypt! Or would that we had died in this wilderness! Why is the LORD bringing us into this land, to fall by the sword? Our wives and our little ones will become a prey. Would it not be better for us to go back to Egypt?' And they said to one another, 'Let us choose a leader and go back to Egypt.'" God's desire for us is given in Philippians 2:15, "that you may be blameless and innocent, children of God without blemish in the midst of a crooked and twisted generation, among whom you shine as lights in the world," yet, instead, we've twisted and bent with society. Paul warns us of the judgment that comes on such people by means of the gospel in 1 Corinthians 1:19, "For it is written: 'I will destroy the wisdom of the wise; the intelligence of the intelligent I will frustrate" (NIV).

As Paul writes, their journeys and their struggles were written as a warning to us. In 1 Corinthians 10:1-13, he gives the full explanation: "For I do not want you to be unaware, brothers, that our fathers were all under the cloud, and all passed through the sea, and all were baptized into Moses in the cloud and in the sea, and all ate the same spiritual food, and all drank the same spiritual drink. For they drank from the spiritual Rock that followed them, and the Rock was Christ. Nevertheless, with most of them God was not pleased, for they were overthrown in the wilderness. Now these things took place as examples for us, that we might not desire evil as they did. Do not be idolaters as some of them were; as it is written, 'The people sat down to eat and drink and rose up to play.' We must not indulge in sexual immorality as some of them did, and twenty-three thousand fell in a single day. We must not put Christ to the test, as some of them did and were destroyed by serpents, nor grumble, as some of them did and were destroyed by the Destroyer. Now these things happened to them as an example, but they were written down for our instruction, on whom the end of the ages has come. Therefore let anyone who thinks that he stands take heed lest he fall. No temptation has overtaken you that is not common to man. God is faithful, and he will not let you be tempted beyond your ability, but with the temptation he will also provide the way of escape, that you may be able to endure it."

Every time Moses cries out to the Lord, the Lord answers him and shows him the way. Moses just asks and waits expectantly. What causes Moses to understand this and not the congregation of Israel? Moses understood God's care for those who are suffering, as expressed in Exodus 22:27b, "And if he cries to me, I will hear for I am compassionate." The reaction of the enemies of God when a suffering person cries out is to disregard or to impose even more burdens and affliction (Exodus 5:8). God, however, hears and moves in compassion. The intent of the testing is so the people of Israel know that God is the LORD their God (Exodus 16:12) who knows them, loves them, and cares for them. But it is also so we know God. These words are documented to warn us and teach us. The glorious tabernacle is a legacy and heritage passed down from believer to believer. God allows us the privilege to endure, to make a life-giving mark in another's life. I cannot help but consider what caused the difference in the faithfulness of Moses and the unfaithfulness of the people of Israel. What will my life produce? The uncertainty of my ongoing faithfulness keeps me clinging to God. *Protect me from my own blindness. Reveal yourself to me. Show me who You made me to be. Let me see You, so I can know You. Know me so I will follow You. Send me to make You known.*

Seeing this change in the Israelites and hearing about their gratitude—which was expressed in generosity so abundant it had to be restrained—caused me to focus for an entire day on showing generosity whenever an opportunity came my way, to gauge how often I restrain my generosity. How would I see the hoarding and the selfishness that come so naturally to me? How would this recognition change me? The first thing I realized was the level of vigilance and awareness it took to look for every opportunity. Shockingly, I realized how much of my day is spent with no awareness of what is going on around me, of just how focused I am on me and on what I need to accomplish.

I started considering what I hoard. I realized that I can be so stingy with what is mine! I can so easily withhold my love and pleasure from people. I am selfish with my time, my money, my family, my acts of service, my affection, my attention, and my testimony. What new opportunities would I see that I have never been aware of if I were not stingy? Like Miriam, whose actions displayed her concern for Moses (Exodus 2:4), how can I be generous by investing in someone else's story? I also considered the opposite view. What am I generous with that I need to restrain? That list was not much better. At times, I am generous with my opinion. All too often, I am generous with my frustration and my displeasure. I could instead choose to be generous with God's words. I could be generous with His mercy, His forgiveness, and His grace.

I realized that my hoarding often has to do with fear and my posture towards God. My giving nature was abused and taken advantage of. If I do not stand up for myself, no one will stand up for me. Some who have claimed to love me have taken advantage of my giving nature. Is God enough for me that I can let go of the pain of the past and trust Him to move forward? Do I trust that He knows me and moves to do what is best for me and others? Nahum 1:7 says, "The LORD is good, a stronghold in the day of trouble; he knows those who take refuge in him." Do I view what He has given me as mine or as something that He has entrusted to me? God has given so generously to us for us, in turn, to be generous. Do I dare to ask, What lies am I believing about God? *God, help me experience Your truth to know You more. Reveal the truth of my heart to me. Help me understand why I clutch onto certain things. What do I need to learn?*

I considered how unrestrained generosity flows from within and is not measured only in the handing over of material things. It is like the woman wiping the feet of Jesus in Matthew 26. Her generosity was twofold. The bottle of perfume was extremely expensive, but the generosity of her heart towards Jesus was in her humility. She used her hair, which was her glory, to wipe his feet. This displayed a bigger and better generosity, an overwhelming generosity and gratitude of her heart. It is an expression of generosity out of the abundance given to us by God to give even that which is not plentiful in our lives. Generosity is best displayed not in giving of the surplus but in giving out of the lack. See Jesus's words when He saw a woman giving all she had at the temple. They are found in Mark 12:42–44: "And a poor widow came and put in two small copper coins, which make a penny. And he called his disciples to him and said to them, 'Truly, I say to you, this poor widow has put in more than all those who are contributing to the offering box. For they all contributed out of their abundance, but she out of her poverty has put in everything she had, all she had to live on.'" Generosity is viewing God in His rightful spot far above the heavens, in His radiant goodness, as the one who deems us worthy to care for, shelter, and protect. It is a heart posture that knows that God supplies all I have, that this God who bestows is all that I need, and that He is enough for me. Pit-dwelling behavior hoards or uses what we have been given for dark purposes. We are instead supposed to consider the lilies of the field and God's care of them (Matthew 6:28) so we may be motivated to store up for ourselves treasures in heaven (Matthew 6:20). God has shown me the overwhelming generosity of others, which has encouraged me to be more generous with my worship, praise, and gratitude. *Through the gratitude and generosity of the Israelites, ordinary things were constructed and used to house the extraordinary. Am I ready to let go of the ordinary to step into the extraordinary?*

One of the first commands Jesus gives to some of His disciples is to "come and see" (John 1:39 KJV). Jesus's last words to His disciples are for them to "go." Matthew 28:19 records this command: "Go therefore and make disciples of all nations, baptizing them in the name of the Father and of the Son and of the Holy Spirit." But in between these two commands is a command for us to follow Him. Matthew 4:19 tells us, "And he said to them, 'Follow me, and I will make you fishers of men.'" I have been pondering the significance of these simple directives and how they relate to a generous spirit. Having a generous spirit means a life of not living for oneself but for others. These commands are significant, and they draw us deeper into the heart of God so that we become more invested in ministering for God. Our following Jesus must result in going, for God is a sending God. Jesus speaks of this in John 17:3, "And this is eternal life, that they know you, the only true God, and Jesus Christ whom you have sent." Isaiah encountered God, and, directly after his unclean lips were cleansed with hot coals, he was ready to go. Isaiah said, "Here am I. Send me" (Isaiah 6:8 NIV). What other response is there after an encounter with our holy God?

~

What a blessed year of God showing me similarities to Moses, not because I have led a multitude to deliverance but because, like Moses, I doubt myself and my abilities, and it causes me to doubt God, and I delay in obeying His purposes for me! I relate to Moses; I feel like a woman of uncircumcised lips. I say that I trust that God can do anything, except when it comes to His ability to use me for his purposes. Like Moses, I question, What if no one listens to me? I worry that I will not know what to say. I struggle to recall simple words, or I say completely the wrong thing. I struggle to articulate what is inside my brain. Somehow, wires get crossed from my brain to my mouth. My family has affectionately labeled it "Angie speak." But the most crippling challenge of all is that I think differently than other people and I struggle to relate to them. Truth is, I perceive that many would consider me weird and vanilla. I am not very exciting. I am not witty, funny, or adventurous. I am not a great conversationalist. Yet when I focus on all these things that I cannot do, my focus is on myself when God is trying to teach me that I am not, but HE IS. What a blessed year of God showing me that, like Moses, my purposes are not bound by my limitations but, by God's power, once I stop looking at myself and start living for Him, once I am focused on obedience to His ways and meeting the needs of others, my life is oriented toward a holy calling and purpose! I am transformed to be generous of heart, overflowing with gratitude and love.

Because of the glory of God filling the tabernacle and because of Moses requesting to see the glory of God, what I have been specifically pondering this year has been to understand more fully the glory of God. To begin to comprehend the glory of God is to realize that His glory is too good and too gentle for me to fully comprehend. My offering is meager, but He provides the opportunity through His perfect plan. He looks upon my offering, which falls so short. He looks upon me, who begins doing for His glory but somehow always manages to turn around and make it about myself, with smiling, beaming favor. He rewards me for it and lavishes His delight and favor upon me. One of the three recent events where I spoke of God's transformation of my life was a live event. Sitting in the back of the room was an authority figure in my life whom I greatly admire for his humility. As I tried to boldly speak up about my past pain and the healing that is offered by my loving Savior, this person was smiling widely and nodding emphatically in the back of the room. I could see the pride in his eyes. It was such an encouragement to have this demonstrative affirmation as I was venturing down a path of boldness and vulnerability in this new way. After the event, I shared the details with a friend. I shared just how meaningful and needed that show of support and favor was. I explained how it encouraged me to be even bolder. Her response still brings a smile to my face. She said that God uses ordinary people to show us His pleasure with our obedience and that this was the favor of Jesus shining through this man. It brought tears to my eyes because she gave me a precious visual of Jesus beaming at me, grinning from ear to ear, with pride and joy shining out of His eyes at me, for something that falls so short in comparison to what He has done for me.

According to the Gospel Coalition, the glory of God is the magnificence, worth, loveliness, and grandeur of God's many perfections.[1] It is the shining forth or the public display of God's character or nature. Simply put, it is when things are the way they were meant to be. If you want to see and experience the glory of God in your life, be known. Step into the light and become who God designed you to be. God's glory was shining through this man at that event. The perfect, righteous, and all-powerful God who laid the Egyptians low was gentle and encouraging towards me, so much so that He took one small event and displayed His glory and His pleasure towards my offering through the actions of someone else. The mighty I AM is the gentle, lowly, and glorious King of Kings.

I also relate to Moses because I have experienced God changing the cadence and rhythm of my life. In John 10:10, Jesus says, "The thief comes only to steal and kill and destroy. I came that they may have life and have it abundantly." Abundant life sounds heavenly! Do you ever read a verse, and it just strikes you? This verse came to me at the very moment in my life where I was experiencing what a "true" life of abundance is *not*, but I could not explain, nor could I recognize what a life of abundance in Christ *was*. This is the cadence that God has placed on my life, a longing and a desire to understand what an abundant life in Christ looks like. How abundant is your life today? Are you worn, tired, or discouraged? Do you long for a taste of His abundance?

For so many years I did not recognize God's rhythmic call. I was too busy trying to be everything for everyone, too busy building my own kingdom. But when we stop and seek Him, He reveals Himself to us and

---

1. Christopher Morgan, "The Glory of God," The Gospel Coalition, January 14, 2020. https://www.thegospelcoalition.org/essay/the-glory-of-god/?queryID=36065e07b9ed ab5bf68e97549fa908d9

indelibly changes us. The first time that I remember hearing God's cadence in my life was in the study of the book of John, when I got to the point where Jesus promises abundant life. This promise of a life of abundance called to me because I was existing, not living. I was not experiencing His abundance. I asked God to show me what His abundance looked like, and my cadence began. As I prayerfully considered what I should meditate on for the upcoming year, the concept of an abundant life was constantly on my heart. As the new year began, my church started a new study in the book of John, and the word *life* was boldly displayed as the backdrop of the sanctuary for that year. Shortly after, I began reading "Sacred Rhythms" by Ruth Haley Barton, and I was encouraged to create a breath prayer, a prayer which has continued for years. My breath prayer is, "Breath of Life, show me Your abundant life." I would pray this request like breathing in and out, desiring it with every fiber of my being. I would pray, "Take my desires, my distractions, and my fears until I understand what your abundance looks like in my life, because without it, my life is empty. I am tired of being the shell of who I am meant to be. I am tired of shadow living." Further fueling the hunger in my soul was the fact that I questioned whether I even knew my Savior's voice. Sometimes it was loud and clear, and at other times I, in confusion, questioned if it was His voice, my voice, or Satan's voice. I was tentative and hesitant. *Lord, let me know You. Let me hear Your voice and move with You—follow You.* I learned that an abundant life does not mean gaining worldly abundance, but rather that living for Christ in gratitude and communing in relationship with Him creates an indescribable joy and brings life to our weary souls that propels us to share this joy with others. He has moved so abundantly in my life that, in Him, I am able to set aside my fears of failure and, instead, to share the truth of God, to speak boldly and authentically of the joy that comes from God's abundance in our lives.

PAUSE TO PRAISE AND PONDER:

Theme: God dwells with us, and we can experience His glory in any situation.
Read Exodus 40:34.

Praise: How have you experienced the glory of God? How have you come to understand the fear of the Lord? How can you bring Him praise?

Brainstorming:

- How am I choosing to be stationary and comfortable, although God is calling me to move?
- How am I moving, although God is calling me to be still and know that He is God?
- In what ways am I too comfortable?
- In what ways am I uncomfortably moving forward in faith?
- How am I resting and abiding in God?

Get Creative:
- Draw a fishbowl with a fish inside the bowl. Draw a second fish outside of the fishbowl. Next to the fish in the fishbowl, write the times you have moved within God's timing. In the fish outside of the fishbowl, write the times you have moved outside of God's timing.
- Draw a tent. Outside the tent, write ways you are seeking to establish a permanent dwelling place although we are not of this world. Inside the tent, write ways to focus on the eternal over the temporal.

Daily Bread: In what ways can you bring God praise today? What is God teaching you about Himself? How is God calling you to be a part of the body of Christ?

- Draw a drinking glass. Select a verse related to what God has revealed to you today as you pondered that speaks truth about the ways and promises of God.

- Draw a sandwich.
    - On the bottom bun, praise God by writing how you know that God dwells with you.
    - In the meat section of the sandwich, write one way that you feel God is calling you to rest and abide, then write a way that you feel God is calling you to move.
    - On the top bun, write a truth contained in God's Word that speaks to abiding in God and write a truth contained in God's Word about walking with Him.

9

ABUNDANT MESSENGER

Once we come and see, once we taste that the Lord is good and feel life breathed into us, and once we rely on the truth of God's words, He calls us to go deeper in relationship with Him. He bestows upon us a more intimate invitation of "Follow Me!" We find an example in Mark 1:17: "And Jesus said to them, 'Follow me, and I will make you fishers of men.'" When we follow and lay claim to this gift, we finally see Him fulfill His promise that we will be His own treasured possession. We know Him more and understand that our standing in Him is based on His foundation. His foundation is secure and unshakable no matter how wobbly and weak our legs are. We rest in Him. What a joyous and blessed place! We belong. But God does not stop there. Our journey continues. For God is building a nation of holy priests. The comfort we receive from Him has a purpose—we receive it so we can go and comfort others. God teaches us His ways and transfers to us His calling—to go and rescue as we have been rescued! He sends us with the same command He gave the Israelites, "arise and go," to find His lost sheep and love them. We find our version of this command in Matthew 28:19-20: "'Go therefore and make disciples of all nations, baptizing them in the name of the Father and of the Son and of the Holy Spirit, teaching them to observe all that I have commanded you. And behold, I am with you always, to the end of the age.'" With delight, we are called. Our walk with God, who we behold as dwelling on the mountaintop of Zion, high and mighty, is found most readily in the pit that He pulled us from because His rescue work is still underway. Sometimes, we hesitantly begin working with Him on something that we are privileged to be a part of. We are selected

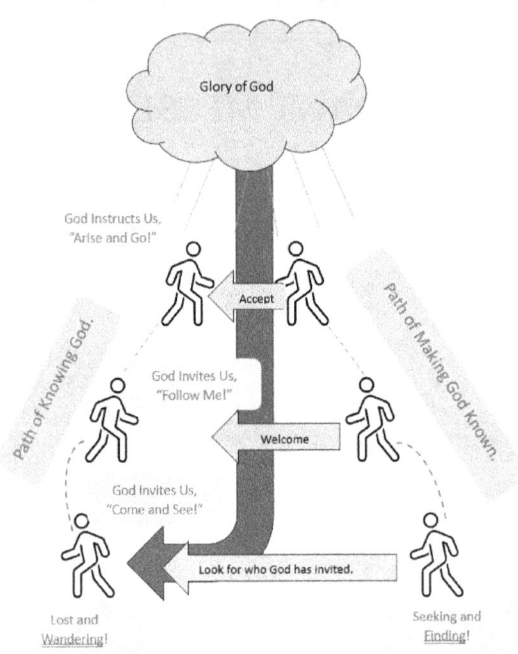

as part of God's search-and-rescue team, but He does not do this because we have any special talents. He lacks nothing. He does not need us for such a crucial , life-or-death operation. He uses us because, through this mission, we grow in the likeness of His Son. It is for our benefit and our delight that He uses us. We grow in His love. We learn by caring about what He cares about and by living out the mission for which He died. Once we are rescued by Him, we are called to walk in obedience, to follow His calling. We see. We trust. We follow. We are to make the good news known, to invite, to welcome, and to accept.

Our journey, however, is not usually so simple. Obeying the call to remain steadfast is brutal because our walk is consistently racked with the challenge of choice. We resist God's calling. We get scared. We turn back and then repent. We are so complex that it is difficult for us to sort out our own feelings and emotions. We hide parts of ourselves from God. Maybe more accurately, we deny parts of our weaknesses and sinfulness to ourselves while actively laying other areas of our lives down to God. We may think we are handing things over to God, while we blindly retain control without even recognizing it. *God continues to mine our hearts to reveal to us where fear and defiance remain within them.*

I wish I was the type of person that could just take the imperative commands within the Bible and do them—not overthink anything, but in joy and obedience just follow the commands of God in sincerity and authenticity. So many times, I see the words "Do not fear" and I shake my head *yes*, determined to follow through, longing to be obedient. I pray, *God, I will do my best to trust You and not be fearful.* Meanwhile, I continue to make decisions that are rooted in fear that I am not even aware that I possess. I'd love to be able to hold and move forward steadfastly, but I know that I do not follow God's call for two reasons: fear and defiance. I am certain one of these two pesky attributes is the root of all these barriers. That is not how my brain works, however. I'm left knowing this simple thought is true but left not knowing how to then fully apply that truth to my life, and this lack of knowledge leaves me frustrated with myself. For human beings, I am not sure there is anything as complex as our emotions, especially the feelings that we've buried within our hearts. Sometimes I'm convinced I'm following God faithfully, only to discover that it is fear driving my actions. Hidden among the good action and good words is sin that I was not aware even existed. At other times, I can recognize that fear is driving me, but I don't know exactly what it is that I'm even afraid of. I just sense danger and fear because I'm apprehensive or defensive and I cannot articulate why. What has been helpful to me is looking at something from another perspective. I find that bringing my confusion and questions before the Lord, curtailing my spiraling and overthinking into meditating on God and His ways, and allowing myself to be searched and known, often brings clarity to the clouds that the simple statement "Do not fear" does not pierce. The following barriers are presented for just such a purpose. These are merely suggestions to consider to help us analyze our hearts and ask God to help us search our hearts for what fear and defiance buried deep within us.

- **Fleshly Weakness Barrier:** One barrier to following God faithfully, to "arising and going" when God calls us, is our flesh. God's grace is vital because our flesh is weak, and, in our weakness, we choose to follow our own desires over being obedient to God. The Bible tells us in 1 Corinthians 10:13, "No temptation has overtaken you that is not common to man. God is faithful, and he will not let you be tempted beyond your ability, but with the temptation he will also provide a way of escape, that you may be able to endure it." Man's character qualities are not conducive to following faithfully. The world leads us astray because we long to be accepted. Our bent is to blame and deny culpability instead of acknowledging our transgressions. Our desires lead us astray, and we choose our pride instead of yielding in humility. We are creatures who find comfort with what we know. We are fearful of what we do not know. Since the world rejects us, in our reluctance to face that rejection, we stutter and stumble instead of gliding forward in confidence. It is in this space of just downright fleshly defiance that my love for Jesus has blossomed, knowing that He chooses me when, in an instant, I am prone to disobey or betray Him. Yet His love for me never wavers. It is that love and grace toward me, based on His goodness instead of my own, that compels me to live differently, to be different. We so often focus our thoughts on *I do not want to do this, God!* when we should ask Him, *God, what am I missing out on due to my selfish, gluttonous, lazy, greedy, or lustful behavior? How are these fleshly desires getting their way affecting my spiritual wellbeing?*

Let me illustrate this with a few examples. The crinkling of a bag drives me crazy. My family knows to grab a handful of chips and put the chips in a bowl if they are in my presence. Why? I have no idea. I know it's the craziest thing to get irritated about, but the sound drives me to level ten irritability on a one to ten irritability scale instantaneously. A crinkling bag is just the first of many things that make me quit being calm and rational. My family could probably make a much more comprehensive list of the things that take me over the edge, but here are just a few:

- So often my children come to me at the last minute for money or supplies for school the next day. Not being a last-minute person, I have a difficult time not showing my irritation and not scolding them about how their emergency is not my problem. While that is understandable, it can get really ugly, however, if they ask for something late into the evening the day before they need it, during that time in the evening just before bed, when I'm tired and I do not want to do anything but relax. I am an early bird. Ask me to do anything in the morning, and I would likely graciously accommodate you. Ask me to do something late in the evening and risk dealing with an extremely grumpy bear. Unfortunately, the grump doesn't only come out of me when my kids are procrastinating. It is known that late evening is my cutoff for any questions, really. One evening, my son approached me, and I got testy. My husband looked at him and said, "You know better than to ask your mom for something after 8:00pm." Wow! That is not what I want to be known for. What I long for and what is real are worlds apart. I don't want my kids to be hesitant to approach me for help, even when they landed themselves in their own mess. I want to be firm, but I also want to be kind. All good intentions quickly fly away, however, in my tiredness.

- Also, I become irritated when the school hands me jobs. A few times my son has tried to let me know that something is coming up that he needs, but I am usually in the middle of something, and I do not want to drop whatever I am doing to take care of it at that moment. Invariably, if I don't take care of it at the time he says something, I end up forgetting about it. If he reminds me, I scold him for badgering me, so there is not a win for him in this. If I dig a little deeper in my heart, I realize that it is not my son's approach that irritates me at all. What I don't like is being given a job by the school. Because I cannot let my kids get bad grades, I am forced to obey the school's rules and I resent being told what to do, when to do it, and how to do it. When I should be modeling respect and responsibility, I model complaining and unhelpfulness.

- Another hot button of mine is being told what to do in a micromanaging way. If you entrust something to me, trust me to get it done, but do not dictate to me how you want me to do it. Sadly, I don't think there is a movie scene that I relate to more than the scene from the movie *Money Pit*, a movie starring Tom Hanks and Shelley Long. In one scene, she asks him to carry up water and then lets him know that the bucket for the water is in the hall. Because he has been doing this job for her every day for months, he already knows where the bucket is. He walks away grabbing the bucket, grumbling, "I know where the bucket is! You don't have to tell me where the bucket is!" Every time I am told how to do something that I already know or anytime someone tries to tell me how to do my job, I find myself muttering under my breath, "I know where the bucket is. You don't have to tell me where the bucket is." For twenty years my husband has heard me mutter, "I know where the bucket is." This past weekend, my family and I headed up to Lake Erie to open our summer trailer. I had to mop the floor, and I grabbed a bucket from the bathroom that was way too small for the mop. Since the floor is tiny, I made do with my makeshift floor bucket but told my husband that I wasn't sure what happened to the bucket that I usually used and asked him to grab a new bucket when he went to the store. He opened the pantry in the kitchen and pointed to the bucket and said, "It's right here," followed by saying with a smirk, "So... You want me to tell you where the bucket is?" Well played Sir!

- **Comfort Barrier:** As we grow closer to God, we grow closer to one another, and we may not even consider seeking to welcome others when our need for community has been met. We are creatures wired to continue with what is comfortable. We find comfort with our brothers and sisters in Christ, so instead of

> arising and going, we retreat and cluster together as believers. We backpedal, feed our own needs, and deem our own worth and identity instead of looking to the needs of others and using our identities to further God's call. In the community of believers, we have not only drawn closer to God but also closer to one another. To leave the comfort of like-mindedness and understanding and pursue people of the world who might reject us or persecute us is risky. If our hearts are asking God to intimately search us, we may discover that although we thought we were yielded and following Christ, we instead find a new wave of recognition of our heart's defiance— the realization that we most often only follow to our level of comfort. We must learn to venture forward in faith. As God draws us deeper, we find relinquishing gets more personal and more difficult.

Too often, we get complacent and forget that God is a sending God as we bask in the blessedness of being known by Him. Just as we were lost and wandering and needed someone to point the way, we should seek to point the way for the lost. Just as we needed someone to invite us to "come and see" the goodness of God, we need to invite others to see Him. We should welcome them, modeling with grace how God invites us no matter how we have sinned. Just like God called us to "Follow Him" and we needed others to accept us and encourage us, we should be accepting others and encouraging them, giving them a place to belong in God's church. We are driven by a desire for normalcy and comfort. I believe in God, but I do not want any storms or difficulties in my life, so where does that leave me?

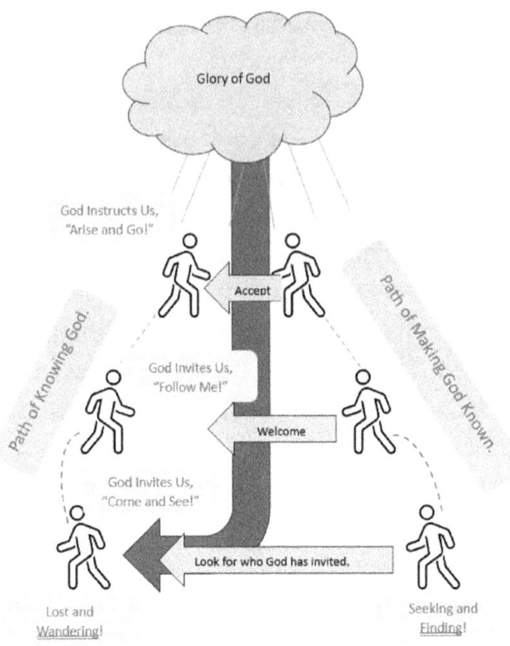

There is something so comforting for us in the community of believers. We've grown closer to one another and closer to God. We belong. It's like we are on a plateau eating up the joy and freedom, the blessing and abundance, but we forget that there are still many in the pit. We balk against leaving our places of comfort for the worldly pit. It is as far away from abundant freedom as we can imagine. It feels as if God is cutting away our blessings and our friendships as He sends us back to the rank, putrid, and cavernous pit. But our sending God sends us to find the lost and wandering to invite and welcome them to come and see, to accept those who desire to follow Him and to encourage those who belong to arise and go. *God, what good things that you have bestowed on me am I unwilling to relinquish, so that they prevent me from arising and going?*

As my company was preparing to interview for a building project, those attending and speaking at the interview were gathered in a conference room to practice going through the presentation. When my slides came up, I took the remote and began going through my part. This was the first time I had ever used this remote. I have been going to interviews for three years, and for three years we have used the same one. The remote in my hand felt foreign and uncomfortable. It did not feel the same. The buttons were not in the same place. It just felt off, unnatural. As I transitioned the slide forward, everything on the screen went black. I cried out, "What happened?" Turns out, I accidentally hit two buttons at once on the remote and that stopped the entire presentation.

It does not take much for my mind to stress about what could go wrong. My mind focuses automatically on everything that could make me look foolish. *What if I trip? What if I get dizzy? What if I stumble over my words? What if I call someone by the wrong name? What if I forget what to say?* Now, I could add a new worry to my list. *What if I shut down the entire slide show in the middle of our presentation?* The morning of the interview, my coworker, who was aware of my concerns, kindly assured me that she grabbed the trusty remote that we always use. How the room was oriented—the location of the monitors in relation to the people interviewing us—did not matter. Only that familiar little gadget in my hand brought me comfort and gave me the confidence to believe that I could do it. Then, the dreaded words came from the client: "You cannot use your laptop. You will need to use a Zip drive and plug into our computer. Here is our remote." *NO! All my confidence removed with one sentence.* Once again, my coworker came through. She asked and managed to swap out the remotes so the steady, comfortable, and faithful one was in my hand once again.

Our qualifications for doing a job well do not rest in our presentation progression skills. In my mind, however, my confidence grew with the familiar object that was grasped in my hand. Isn't that just like us? We want to remain in our comfort. We want to know what we are doing. We want to be confident with it. We want to hold onto something as if we are in control even if that control is an illusion. We think selfishly, *God, let me grasp what brings me comfort. Let me remain in comfortable places doing comfortable things. Even knowing you are with me, being held in Your righteous right hand still feels precarious. I would rather latch onto this false sense of security than learn about real peace and comfort in You.* In reality, what is familiar is what is precarious. No matter how much we plan and rehearse, we are not in control. Changes can come more quickly than we are able to respond to them. God rarely leaves us in a comfortable place for too long. We are led in the wilderness or through the valley of the shadow of death, through hard places, not familiar places. But He provides for us, remains with us, and protects us along the way. We discover Him and grow to know Him and rely on Him in our need in ways that we could never discover, know, or rely on Him in our place of comfort. Why? Because we grow to understand and trust Him as our Comfort. Often, our prayers and our desires for healing are solely focused on ourselves, and God's will for our lives is not even a factor. Truthfully, sometimes the circumstances and the grief are too heavy to even consider anything beyond just getting through the day. We need others to step into our grief and hold us up in prayer because we are just too weary. Like Aaron and Hur did for Moses, we need to hold up the arms of those around us as they grow weary. We think, *I just want to let this go. I cannot carry it any longer. I do not want to be stretched or pruned. I do not want to grow. I just want You to remove it from me, so I can go back to being in control of my life.* Instead, we should be asking, *God, how do You want me to move in this circumstance? How are You moving? Move me to trust You.*

• **Knowledge Barrier:** Since this book is all about our knowledge problem, naturally one of the most difficult barriers we face, which impedes us from maturing in our faith, coincides with our knowledge problem. It is a barrier that comes from an improper view of the balance between God and ourselves. As we discovered throughout this book, we have a knowledge problem in a myriad of ways:

• Chapter 1—It is often only in hindsight that we see and know how God is leading us on **"The Beautiful Path."** Our story and our journey do not end with deliverance but God is leading us to a land of abundance and teaching us how to be citizens in His kingdom.

• Chapter 2—We view ourselves as **"Kings and Slaves"** and don't understand our value and worth in comparison to a holy God. We neither understand how we have landed ourselves in a pit separated from God as we demand to rule over our own lives nor can we see the purposes God has created us to fill as we wallow in shame.

• Chapter 3—Then our Creator God, the mighty **"I Am,"** makes Himself known. He invites us to come and see His steadfast love and mercy. He reveals Himself to us and offers to rescue us from our sin.

• Chapter 4—God knows us and reveals to us that we are **"Called by Name"** to leave the pit and follow Him, and no amount of frailty or weakness can keep us from fulfilling the purposes God prepared for us to accomplish in prosperity.

• Chapter 5—God makes known to us the lies surrounding what we hold as the source of our worth and identity. We learn our freedom is to be used for a specific purpose, to bring honor and glory to God. We learn to lay down our false identities, and we learn the value of **"Laying Down the Serpent."**

• Chapter 6—By **"Catching the Serpent by the Tail,"** God makes known to us the unfailing power and prosperity of our identities when we remain within His plan for our lives, even as we grasp onto the risky, scary, and unknown. He directs us to arise and go to rescue others.

• Chapter 7—We come to know the unwavering faithfulness and goodness of God in the journey through **"The Vast Wilderness."** God reveals Himself in the difficult spaces more than in the land flowing with milk and honey. There is beauty found in broken spaces, and we learn to trust in His provision and that God is sufficient *because we discover that He is all we need.*

• Chapter 8—We come to understand that the blessing of God's favor is from His presence in **"The Glorious Tabernacle"** and not from any wealth or prosperity that He bestows. He comes down and dwells with us. The contrast is never greater than when the glorious and the extraordinary dwell in magnificent beauty in the barren and desolate.

The biggest struggle for me was never what was going to be included in the pages of this book. I found structuring it to be the most challenging part of writing. Each of these struggles that I have described is a standalone deficiency in our sight and our comprehension. The book is laid out as a linear explanation of the various facets that we lack and need to have to solidify our faith, yet there is a deeper level of understanding that comes with viewing each of these elements from the perspective of the others. We can know that God is pretty great, but sometimes, we think we're pretty great too. So even though we *know* His goodness, we do not fully appreciate His goodness, because both our goodness in comparison to Him and our understanding of our goodness in comparison to His understanding of our goodness are skewed. Knowing ourselves and the true condition of our hearts is also so important. But not understanding how He changes our condition impedes our ability to move forward with confident knowledge about what He created us to do. Back and forth I went, trying to discern where to begin, not knowing which knowledge problem begins the wreckage. I found myself writing the middle chapters first and branching backwards and forwards from the middle to get past this block of which knowledge problem was most important to convey first. Why was it so hard for me? Because transformation truly takes having the proper balance of knowing who we are in comparison to God, who we are without God, and who we are in God. I knew the shame of being sinful and not being enough, but it made me try even more to be worthy of God's favor. It was not until I understood that God, in his glorious perfection, willingly and fully covers my unworthiness— that He sees me as worthy and gives me purpose because of Jesus Christ alone—it is only when I had this proper balance of understanding Who God is and what He was willing to do for me, who I was and how undeserving I was of that gift, and who I've become due to that gift, that my heart started to transform.

Here are some other versions of the knowledge problem that has been a theme of this book:

- **Viewing God too loftily:** If we view God too loftily, we recognize God as Creator but don't see Him as the God who draws near in rescue—we don't allow Him to guide and direct us. We inaccurately view Him as mighty but withdrawn, uncaring, and cold. When we consider only His justice and His might, and miss His grace and His mercy, we risk viewing Him as so high in the heavens that He is unreachable, untouchable, uncaring, and distant. Jesus brought himself low in both His birth and in His death. There was nothing special about Him (Isaiah 53:2b) in His flesh, yet He is Almighty God. If I was going to present myself to someone, I would want to make the best impression. I would buy a new outfit. I would carefully put on my makeup and do my hair. I would want to look and feel my best, so I am at my most confident. I would want to impress whoever I am meeting. Jesus was concerned only with the will of the Father—serving and saving. This God in the clouds, Who is so vastly superior to us, comes down to show us that He is a God of grace, compassion, and love. But this is not a free love but a jealous love, like that of a spouse who wants their partner to be faithful. *God, I know You are mighty enough to rescue me from the situation, but I so often wonder, will You? Your Word tells me that you* *have plans for me—to prosper me and give me my future. I want to believe that. Are You trustworthy with my heart?*

• **Viewing God too lowly:** If we view God too lowly, we are driven by fear, unable and unwilling to move outside of our comfort zones, because we do not trust that God is in control and that all things occur only within His sovereign will. When we consider only His love, we risk viewing Him as so low that He is our buddy, our pal, but not the Creator of the universe Whom we should fearfully obey. God is both our Lion and our Lamb. We do not keep these truths balanced well. We either view God as loving and passively weak or wrathful and harsh. God will have His justice for every sin committed. The balance is understanding that God is both perfectly hard and perfectly soft simultaneously. His love is soft, kind, compassionate, and merciful and is bestowed because the justice He demands is satisfied through the death of Christ Jesus. His faithfulness is firm, hard, unshakable, steady, and true.

The closer and closer I get to seeing and experiencing God's heart, the further away from His heart I realize that I am. The drastic contrast between His heart and mine becomes more and more apparent, and my gratitude for His faithful loving-kindness grows. I see with more clarity just how far away I am from Him. There is something special in just how unique His heart is, something I think takes us a long time to more fully grasp. We will never completely grasp it. Every time we try to quantify the size of it, we bind it and limit it. Just like the idea of infinity, it needs to be further and further expanded to comprehend its magnitude. It is truly unfathomable. *God, I know You are bigger than my problems. Help me to remember that You rescue me from this and that, if you choose not to, there is a purpose behind every situation that has nothing to do with how much You love me or Your control over creation.*

• **Viewing ourselves too loftily:** If we view ourselves too loftily, if we recognize God as the Creator but do not realize our wicked ways, we are content seeing ourselves as good and dictating our own course. Like the Israelites, we are set apart and favored without a shred of righteousness and very little faithfulness. We are rescued and led into the wilderness to learn about the magnificence of our God in our lack and need. We take God's grace for granted, not truly grateful or thankful for this amazing gift. Even as believers, we all too easily fall into this trap. Sitting in a pious place, judging the actions of others, becomes our way. Grumbling and complaining happen in our hearts. If you look to your circumstances to determine what a sweet, comfortable life looks like, you will spend a lifetime grumbling against someone who is causing your current state. God is a good, benevolent, and present God. He often moves and acts in the hard places, not the smooth ones, so when the difficulties come you have nothing to hold onto, because the promises you believed in are nothing but lies.

A loved one of mine has been pondering the work of the church. She has said to me, "You know, Angie, when we are set free from sin by God, we go to church just to be put back in [legalistic] bondage." Is that *what* we do, church? Oppress? Shame? Bind? Or do we loose? The world certainly thinks we bind. Many believers act as if it is so. Are we a church full of mold fitters giving obligatory sacrifices? We speak of grace, but do our actions scream, "works"? We are great at following external rules, but have we lost our first love and our joy? I have heard so many people say that they would not step foot inside the door of a church because they already know that they would not fit in. Is our mold more important than our love?

We focus on obedience and cut external things from our lives, but God commands His people to *do* as much as He commands us to *not do*. Within God's commands is a call to love Him with all that we are and to have joy and thanksgiving within us. How often do we see this call reflected, shining out of the heart of a believer? It reminds me of God's warning to the church of Laodicea. That warning is found in Revelation 3:15–17: "'I know your works: you are neither cold nor hot. Would that you were either cold or hot! So, because you are lukewarm, and neither hot nor cold, I will spit you out of my mouth. For you say, I am rich, I have prospered, and I need nothing, not realizing that you are wretched, pitiable, poor, blind, and naked.'" Church, is this who we are today? Have we become so complacent because of years of favor from the Lord that we're in danger of practicing idols as the Israelites did just before the Babylonian captivity? *God, show me the depths of my sin, so I can repent and turn back to you with gratitude and joy.*

• **Viewing ourselves too lowly:** If we view ourselves too lowly, we recognize ourselves as sinful but do not recognize that we are new creations in Jesus Christ. God is transforming us. Even as believers, we can fall into this trap. Either we are ineffective for God's purpose for our lives because we are mired down in shame, or we strive to claim our own value and worth, distracted from and oblivious to God's call on our lives. We speak of God's forgiveness, yet we refuse to quit holding ourselves to such high standards or we strive to supplement God's grace with our righteousness, as if what He did on our behalf is not enough.

Isaiah 25:1 says, "O Lord, you are my God; I will exalt you; I will praise your name, for you have done wonderful things, plans formed of old, faithful and sure." These wonderful things include my purpose and your purpose. The important thing is to remember the balance of two truths. The first one is that God's wonderful things are not defined by my wonderful talents and abilities or by the wonderful nature of my life. The second one is that my talents and abilities are bestowed so I can give God honor and glory, and God's plans are wonderful despite the quality of my life here on this earth because we are promised a new city. *God, show me how your rescue of me made me a new creation. Let me see what plans you have in store for me. Show me how the righteous prosper.*

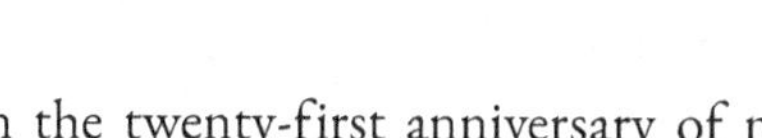

On the twenty-first anniversary of my aunt going home to be with the Lord, her daughter, confessing her struggle with grief, reached out to me while I was deeply engrossed in spreadsheets at work. My first thought was panic, because I was not sure how to respond. I wanted to mourn with her. I wanted to comfort her. I wanted her to know that I saw her and that I heard her and that I wanted to meet her in her pain, but I felt ill-equipped in this endeavor. I was fearful and not sure I could articulate my feelings, let alone bring her comfort. I prayed, *God, I am not equipped to meet her in this place. I do not know what mourning the loss of your mother feels like.* I did not want to pump her full of trite phrases and useless platitudes. Why is our first reaction always about ourselves? As I considered how to respond, the words of the song playing through my headphones struck me: "Just be held. I'm painting beauty with the ashes" from Casting Crowns' song, "Just Be Held." With nothing else to offer and at a loss for words, I acknowledged to her both my lack of words and ability to fully understand her grief. I then told her that my prayer for her is that she would be held and that God would paint beauty with the ashes of her loss.

Her response back to me was a most precious gift that still leaves me a bit speechless. Without my knowledge, God has already used this song in her story to bring her comfort and peace in hard things. You see, her last name, while not spelled the same, is pronounced like "ash." He used the precise moment that I was listening to the song to utter the words that she needed to hear. My words fell so short of what I longed for them to be, but God ensures each small offering is precisely what is needed. They were precisely the words needed to pierce her soul, and, in turn, God pierced mine, the soul of the one who uttered the words.

God could have chosen any number of means and methods to speak truth and encouragement into her heart that day, and He certainly did not need me but He allowed me the honor and privilege to connect with Him and with my cousin. I was able to mourn with her. God blesses beyond comprehension if we only humble ourselves enough to approach him in our lack and become emboldened in His strength. When we serve a God who serves, there is absolutely nothing He needs from us, not even proximity or set plans. He grants us an invitation to step into these beautiful divine appointments, and we can just rest in His goodness. Quite outside of my maneuverings or schemes, God blessed me by allowing me to witness His hand in the little details, showing that He is a God who sees and that He is a God who comforts, and He gave me the privilege of playing a part in it. Isaiah 61:3 (NLT) says, "To all who mourn in Israel, he will give a crown of beauty for ashes, a joyous blessing instead of mourning, festive praise instead of despair. In their righteousness, they will be like great oaks that the Lord has planted for his own glory." My aunt was a model of quiet dignity and taking the awful, heart-wrenching deliveries of life and facing them in God's power, and I see that legacy passed down to her daughters. I have been blessed to be a witness to God in action as He makes beauty from the ashes in my cousin's life, and God is not even done with her or her sister yet. Part of that beauty is that, in the pain and the hardship, my cousin and her sister have patiently endured, being upheld in God the Father.

- **The Barrier of Balance:**

Not only do we need to keep the understanding of who God is and just how precious we are to Him in balance but the Bible is full of other areas that need to be balanced. Here are three areas in which we can all too often adopt an extreme stance that is unyielding and prevents us from moving and seeing God work:

• **Faith and Works**—Have you ever noticed the balance contained within God's Word? For example, Matthew 6 tells us our actions cannot just be for show, but James 2 tells us that our faith, without works, is dead. We simultaneously need to align our inner self and its desires with the rest of our physical bodies—what we do, what we say, and how we love. So, while saving faith cannot be gained through works, it is evidenced by the works we do. Galatians 3:10–13 says, "For all who rely on works of the law are under a curse; for it is written, 'Cursed be everyone who does not abide by all things written in the Book of the Law, and do them.' Now it is evident that no one is justified before God by the law, for 'The righteous shall live by faith.' But the law is not of faith, rather 'The one who does them shall live by them.' Christ redeemed us from the curse of the law by becoming a curse for us—for it is written, 'Cursed is everyone who is hanged on a tree.'" *God, in what ways am I working to gain my own righteousness? How is my faith proving to be dead as I am not fulfilling the work you have entrusted for my life?*

• **Obedience and Tradition**—God desired for His people to intimately know His ways and His laws, to be changed by them, and to diligently teach them to His children. In Deuteronomy 6:6–9, Moses passed down this command from God: "And these words that I command you today shall be on your heart. You shall teach them diligently to your children, and shall talk of them when you sit in your house, and when you walk by the way, and when you lie down, and when you rise. You shall bind them as a sign on your hand, and they shall be as frontlets between your eyes. You shall write them on the doorposts of your house and on your gates." We need to remember why we practice our traditions and follow God's laws to prevent the law becoming what we serve. We can become so focused on the tradition that we cease to remember that it was His strong arm that delivered us and not our adherence to the tradition. *God, in what ways am I going through the motions and not following You, my first love? Lord, what laws have You instilled in me that I am neglecting? How am I not following You in obedience?*

• **Striving and Resting**—God invites us to enter His calling and His mission, but we can move beyond His calling for us and strive to assert our own legacy. Miriam was an example of this. She was a prophetess (Exodus 15:20). In comparison to Moses, her role in Israel's history is small and relatively quiet, yet so important. Ambition and insubordination caused her to be stricken with leprosy. *Lord, how am I jockeying for position like Miriam? How am I moving beyond Your call on my life? How am I not waiting and resting in You? How have I become too complacent and gone from resting to falling asleep? How do I need to be alert and watchful?*

- **Societal Barriers:**

Society has relaxed in many ways regarding what is viewed as sinful and immoral, which means that those who hold to the Word of God are automatically assigned the labels "judgmental" and "intolerant." We have lost our ability to dispute the false belief that speaking truth to a person and condemnation of a person are the same. God's Word shows us that revealing truth is love, not condemnation. *God, what truths am I shying away from because it makes me uncomfortable to share them?* The more, as a society, that we assert that our identity is established by how we feel, the harder it is to claim that God determines our identity without appearing prejudiced and abusive to the world. I think of Jesus and how He navigated difficult situations and got to the heart of people's concerns instead of just physically healing them. He knew their hearts. It is only through the Holy Spirit that we can hope to, with grace and love, speak truth into the hearts of the world. Instead, we try to convince people of the truth in our own power and, as a result, turn people away from God instead of toward Him, or we avoid speaking of God to people entirely.

- **Mindset Barriers:**

One of the barriers to transformation, as we saw in the lives of the Israelites in the wilderness, is forgetting what we should not, which is often connected with remembering inaccurately. God tells them to remember. Exodus 13:3 says, "Then Moses said to the people, 'Remember this day in which you came out from Egypt, out of the house of slavery, for by a strong hand the Lord brought you out from this place.'" As the Egyptians pursue the Israelites to the Red Sea, we see forgetfulness that surfaces in opposite extremes—fear and terror on the one hand and arrogant pursuit on the other. The Israelites had a prime viewing opportunity to watch God eliminate their enemy forever, and fear clouded their sight. The people of Israel forgot that God prevailed against Egypt, not they themselves. Instead of remembering God's mighty arm and trusting Him by being silent, standing firm, and watching the victory of God as the Egyptians drew near, the first of many complaints and accusations against Moses begins, specifically that they would be better off staying in Egypt as slaves (Exodus 14:11–12). Pharaoh forgets what God has done to his nation as he is consumed with not letting the people of Israel go from serving him. God deliberately makes it appear as if the Israelites are trapped in the wilderness to entrap the Egyptians. In Exodus 14:3, God tells Moses that this is exactly what Pharaoh is thinking: "For Pharaoh will say of the people of Israel, 'They are wandering in the land; the wilderness has shut them in.'" Pharaoh is so focused on himself that he cannot see the destruction that he is bringing upon himself and his people until it is too late. The Lord made the Egyptian military understand, however: Exodus 14:25b says, "And the Egyptians said, 'Let us flee from before Israel, for the Lord fights for them against the Egyptians.'"

Perhaps the most grievous example of forgetfulness is when the people of Israel worship the golden calf and attribute their deliverance from the Egyptians to this lifeless god. They forgot that the living God was among them, and they forsook Him for something dead. The Israelites continuously skew their past into a haven because of their fear and something to long for because they want to fill their bellies, when their past was slavery and oppression.

- **Spiral Barriers:**

Another barrier to transformation is the spiral barrier, the unhealthy pattern of replaying in shame or embarrassment what you should have or could have done in a situation that causes you to dwell on that situation and spiral out of control. Self-reflection is not bad, but punishing yourself with regret and walking through a scenario with non-broken, positive outcomes challenges the sovereign plan of God. In a self-destructive thought pattern, we decimate our own worth while, at the same time, arrogantly challenging the truth that God uses all things for His purposes and glory. Do not be swayed by your fears and emotions. Stop trying to grasp and define what you think would be better and quit holding yourself to such high standards. Trust that He has been using all things for the good of those who love Him and those who are called according to his purpose. Just follow Him!

~

I recently had three separate opportunities where I had the privilege of sharing how God has changed my life. For each event, I approached what I would say very differently, going from writing out a script that I practiced but trying to be open to the Spirit editing during the podcast to loosely knowing how I would answer questions but relying on the Spirit to provide the words to say to knowing the topic but focusing the morning of the podcast on writing my personal story in the previous chapter of this book that related to the topic we were discussing. Each approach caused a different critique to surface in my mind. The first critique was that I was too detailed in areas and did not give myself enough time to circle back and explain why I shared the details, which drove me to feelings of fear and condemnation. I was afraid that it came across as rambling without purpose. I was concerned that no one would understand why I gave unnecessary details, or care to hear the words I had to say if they were not perfectly, concisely presented. It led to me replaying the conversation over and over in my head, considering what I should have said differently or what I should have cut out. At the next event, I found myself on the opposite end of the spectrum, but still hyperfocusing. I was so thrilled with the result, playing the conversation over and over in my head, thrilled with my responses and how I was in the zone, being able to provide my testimony in front of my peers. I found myself verging on glorying in the success. While recording the third event, it felt as if God was completely in the conversation with us. The host spoke what God was also laying on my heart, yet I still found myself critiquing. I walked away frustrated with myself that I did not prepare myself enough to speak on such a personal topic, that I was too weepy and too emotional in my delivery. Here are my thoughts that I captured in my journal following the first event.

Speaking of how God has changed my life is a lovely privilege that is incomparable. Instead of joy and satisfaction that he was proclaimed and that the glory was his, I retreat to familiar patterns of focusing on myself and analyzing myself, when the point is to promote Him. Even when I enter each conversation seeking the Spirit's leading, I cannot help but hyperfocus on myself in the aftermath. Why, if I trust God at his word...

Psalm 34:4 (NIV) I sought the Lord and he answered me; he delivered me from all my fears.

Psalm 55:22 (NIV) Cast your cares on the Lord and he will sustain you; he will never let the righteous be shaken.

1 Peter 3:15 but in your hearts honor Christ the Lord as holy, always being prepared to make a defense to anyone who asks you for a reason for the hope that is in you; yet do it with gentleness and respect.

. . . do I question the words that came out of my mouth? As there was calmness and not a doubt of what to say during the recording, why do I doubt what I said after its completion? I have no control or ability to change anything retroactively, so it is a waste of energy and robs me of joy, praise, and thanksgiving. It is giving in to the attack. Instead of humbly professing my gratitude, I am pridefully dissecting my perceived flaws, taking on the angelic persona instead of staying grounded in my identity as a messenger of God. It shows me the importance of handing over my conversations and my opportunities to God as much after they have been completed as when I am in the middle of them. Ephesians 4:32 (NIV) "Be kind and compassionate to one another, forgiving each other, just as in Christ God forgave you." God is teaching me to be kind and compassionate towards myself, while also teaching me that my imperfections and His perfect, sovereign plan work together. He is able and will use my tiny, unworthy offering.

My prayer is that something within this barrier section pricked your heart and niggled at you. Whatever the word or phrase, I pray that you take it to the Lord seeking His wisdom to understand why it impacted you. I pray you come to a greater understanding of who God is and that He gives you a deeper faith to follow Him more faithfully. I pray that you step into what God is calling you to, that you relinquish the fear or the temporal idol you are clutching onto, and that you venture forward in faith, not concerned about success, failure, comfort, or retaliation but with your eyes fixed on the only one who establishes prosperity and grants you the life of abundance that is worthy of being lived in response to the only life that was lived worthy and given for us.

~

PAUSE TO PRAISE AND PONDER:

Theme: What is holding you back from knowing God, being known by God, and making Him known?

Praise: How have you experienced the voice of God while pausing to praise and ponder? How has God made Himself known?

Brainstorming:
Go back over your responses from each chapter. What barriers are holding your back from following God with wholehearted generosity and stepping into the works He has prepared beforehand for us to do?

Get Creative:
- Draw a scale. Consider how God is calling you. Enter the ways you need to remain balanced in your walk on each side of the scale. To the side of the scale, write ways you need to follow with unrestrained generosity.

Daily Bread: In what ways can you bring God praise today? What is God teaching you about following Him?

• Draw a drinking glass. Select a verse related to what God has revealed to you today as you pondered that speaks about the ways and promises of God.

• Draw a sandwich.

◦ On the bottom bun, praise God by writing how you know that God knows you and has called you to make Him known.

◦ In the meat section of the sandwich, write one way that you feel God is calling you and what barrier is holding you back.

◦ On the top bun, write a truth contained in God's Word about abiding in God and write a truth contained in God's Word about walking with Him.

BIBLIOGRAPHY

BlueLetterBible. "H175—'aharon— Strong's Hebrew Lexicon (KJV)." https://www.blueletterbible.org/lexicon/h175/kjv/wlc/0-1/.

BlueLetterBible. "H6326—pû 'â—Strong's Hebrew Lexicon (KJV)." https://www.blueletterbible.org/lexicon/h6326/kjv/wlc/0-1/.

BlueLetterBible. "H8326—šiprâ—Strong's Hebrew Lexicon (KJV)." https://www.blueletterbible.org/lexicon/h8236/kjv/wlc/0-1/.

Lewis, C.S. *God in the Dock.* Edited by Walter Hooper. Grand Rapids, MI: William B. Eerd-mans Publishing Company, 1970.

Morgan, Christopher. "The Glory of God." The Gospel Coalition. January 14, 2020. https://www.thegospelcoalition.org/essay/the-glory-of-god/?queryID=36065e07b9ed ab5bf68e97549fa908d9.

ABOUT KHARIS PUBLISHING

Kharis Publishing, an imprint of Kharis Media LLC, is a leading Christian and inspirational book publisher based in Aurora, Chicago metropolitan area, Illinois. Kharis' dual mission is to give voice to under-represented writers (including women and first-time authors) and equip orphans in developing countries with literacy tools. That is why, for each book sold, the publisher channels some of the proceeds into providing books and computers for orphanages in developing countries so that these kids may learn to read, dream, and grow.

For a limited time, Kharis Publishing is accepting unsolicited queries for nonfiction (Christian, self-help, memoirs, business, health and wellness) from qualified leaders, professionals, pastors, and ministers.

Learn more at: https://kharispublishing.com/

www.ingramcontent.com/pod-product-compliance
Lightning Source LLC
LaVergne TN
LVHW010617100826
845148LV00014B/3012

* 9 7 8 1 6 3 7 4 6 6 8 1 0 *